The Mandala : Coloring Book for Adult

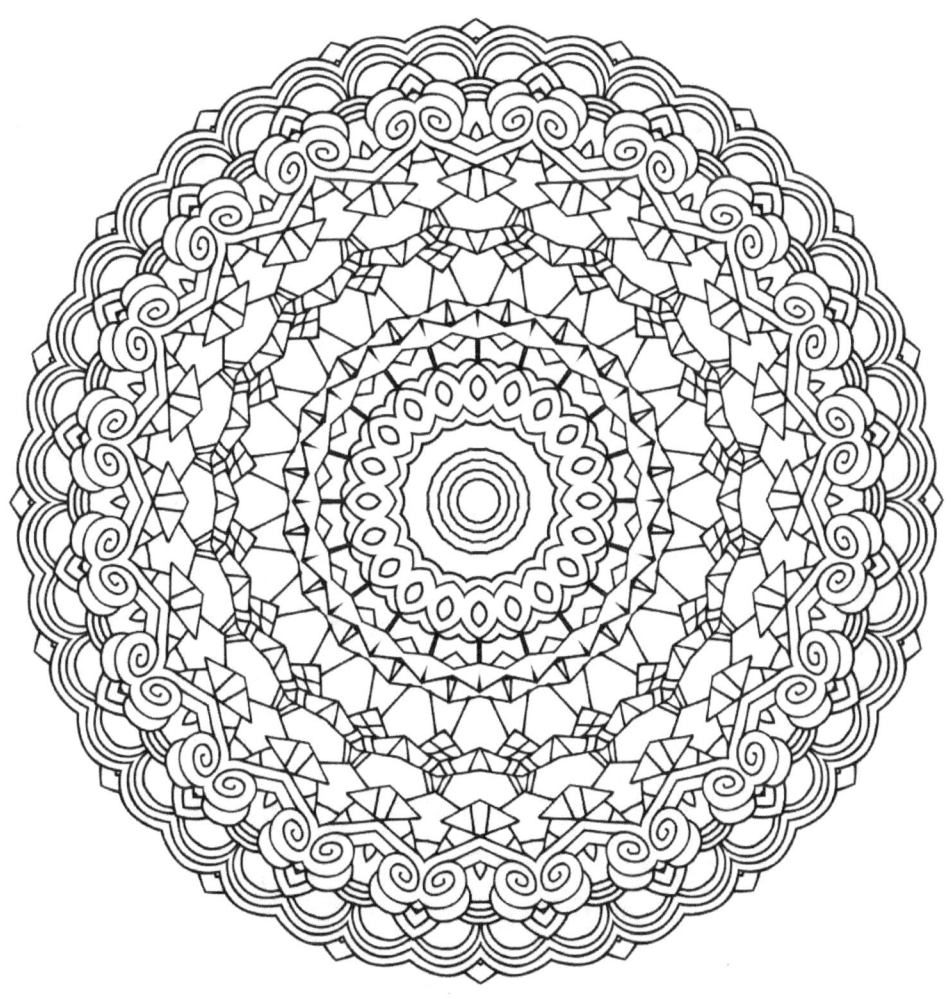

Alin J.

Mandala : Coloring for Stress Relief

Copyright: Published in the United States by Alin J.
Published October 2016

ISBN-13:978-1539704775

ISBN-10:1539704777

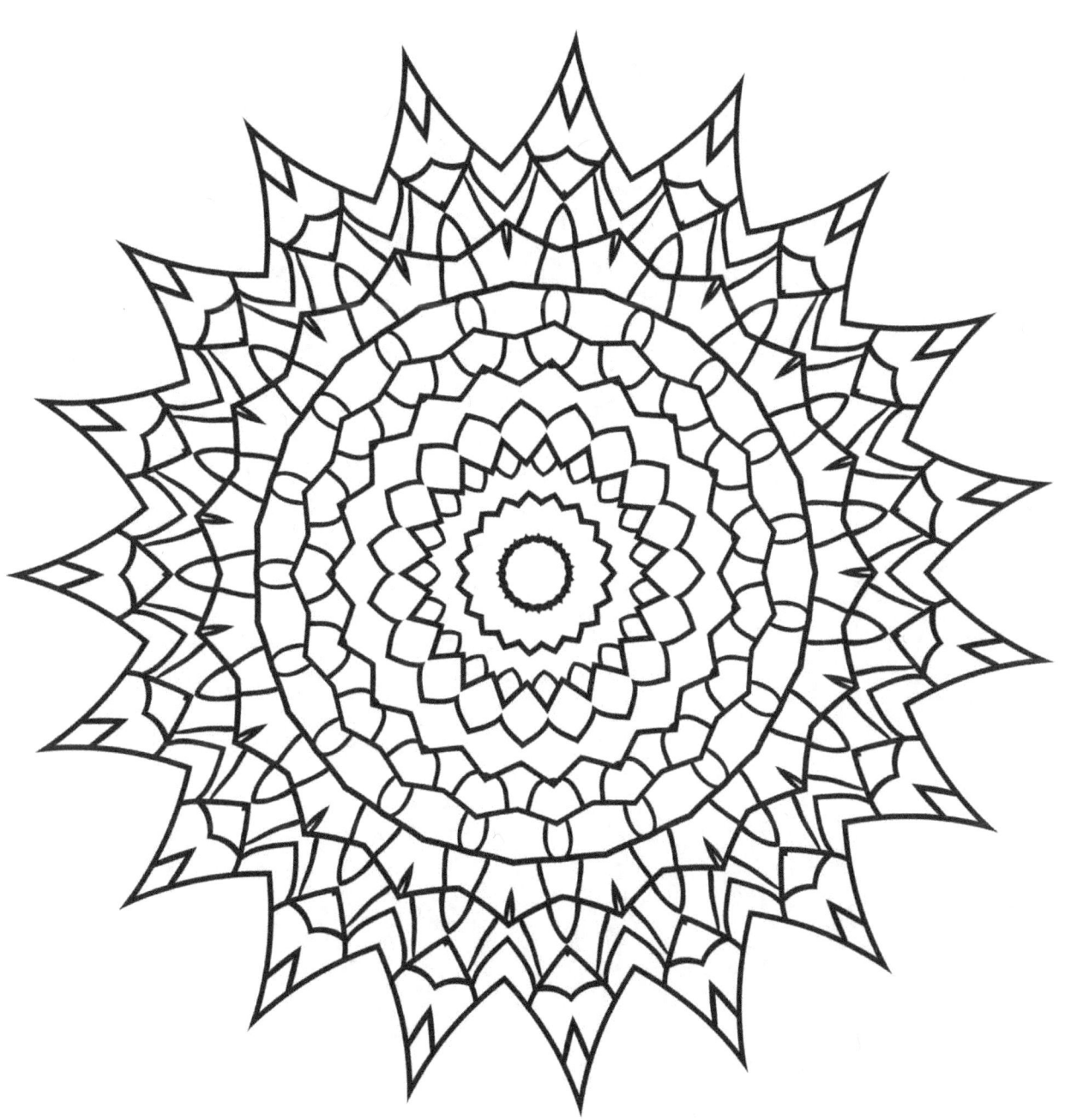

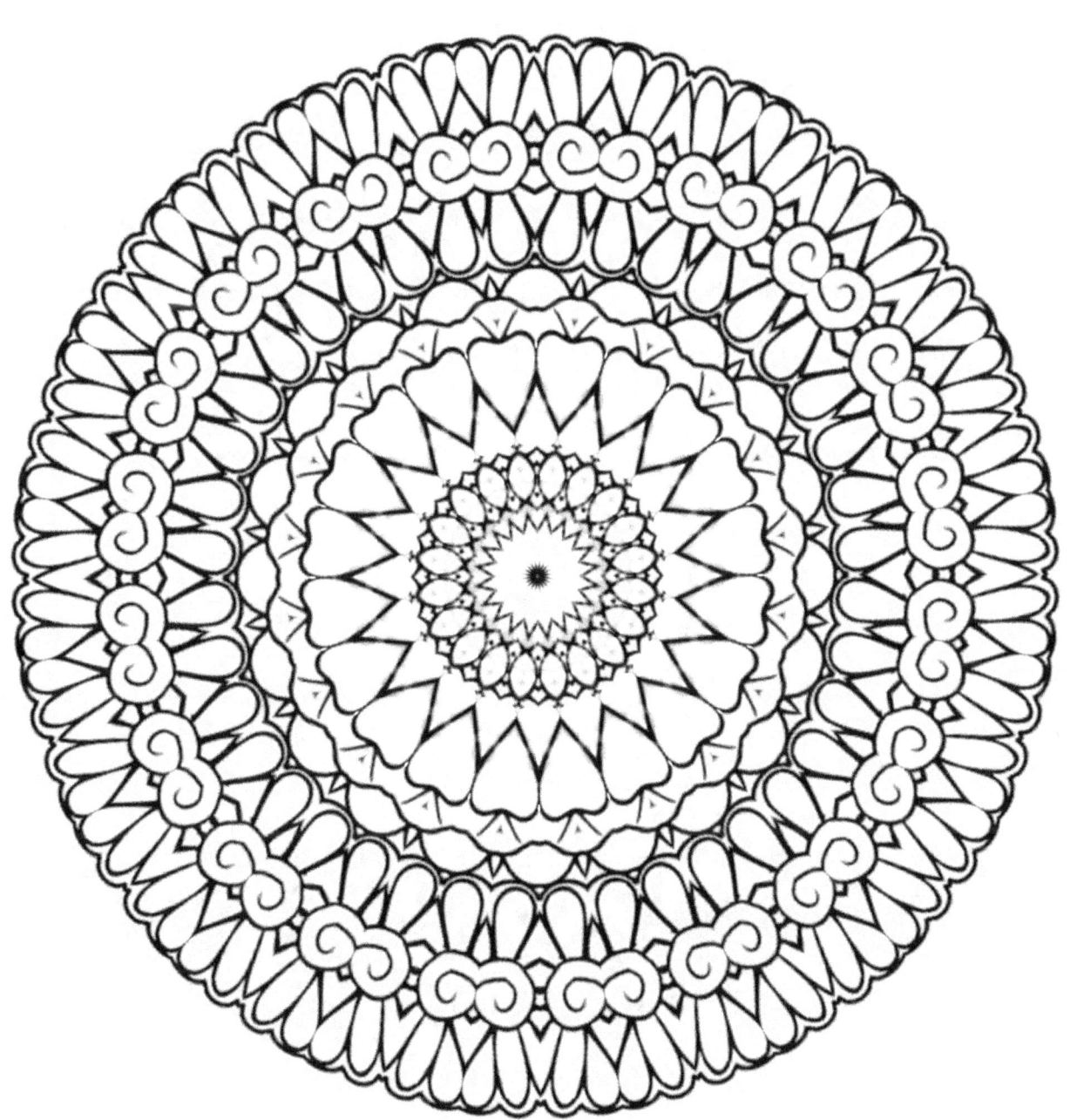

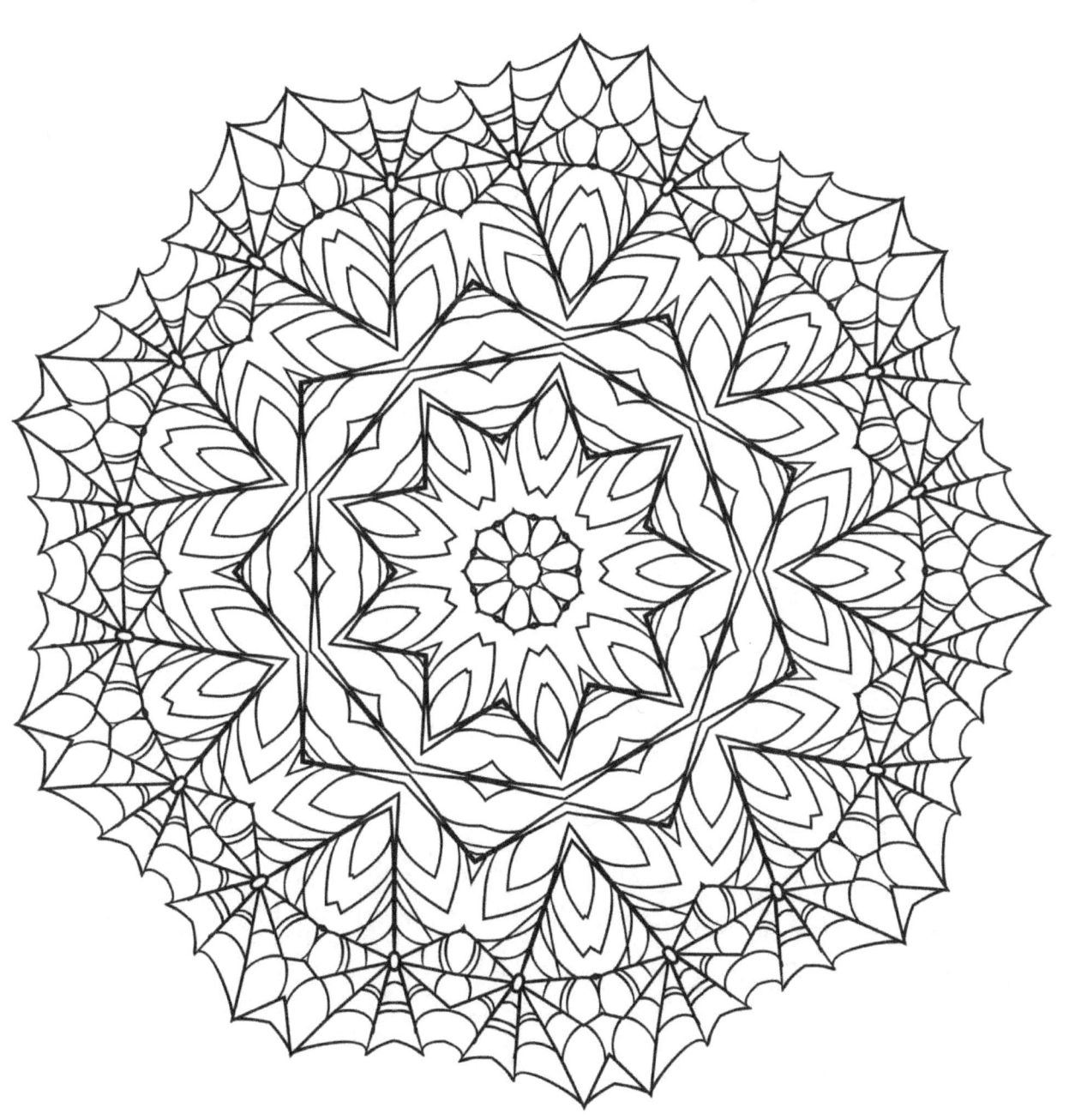

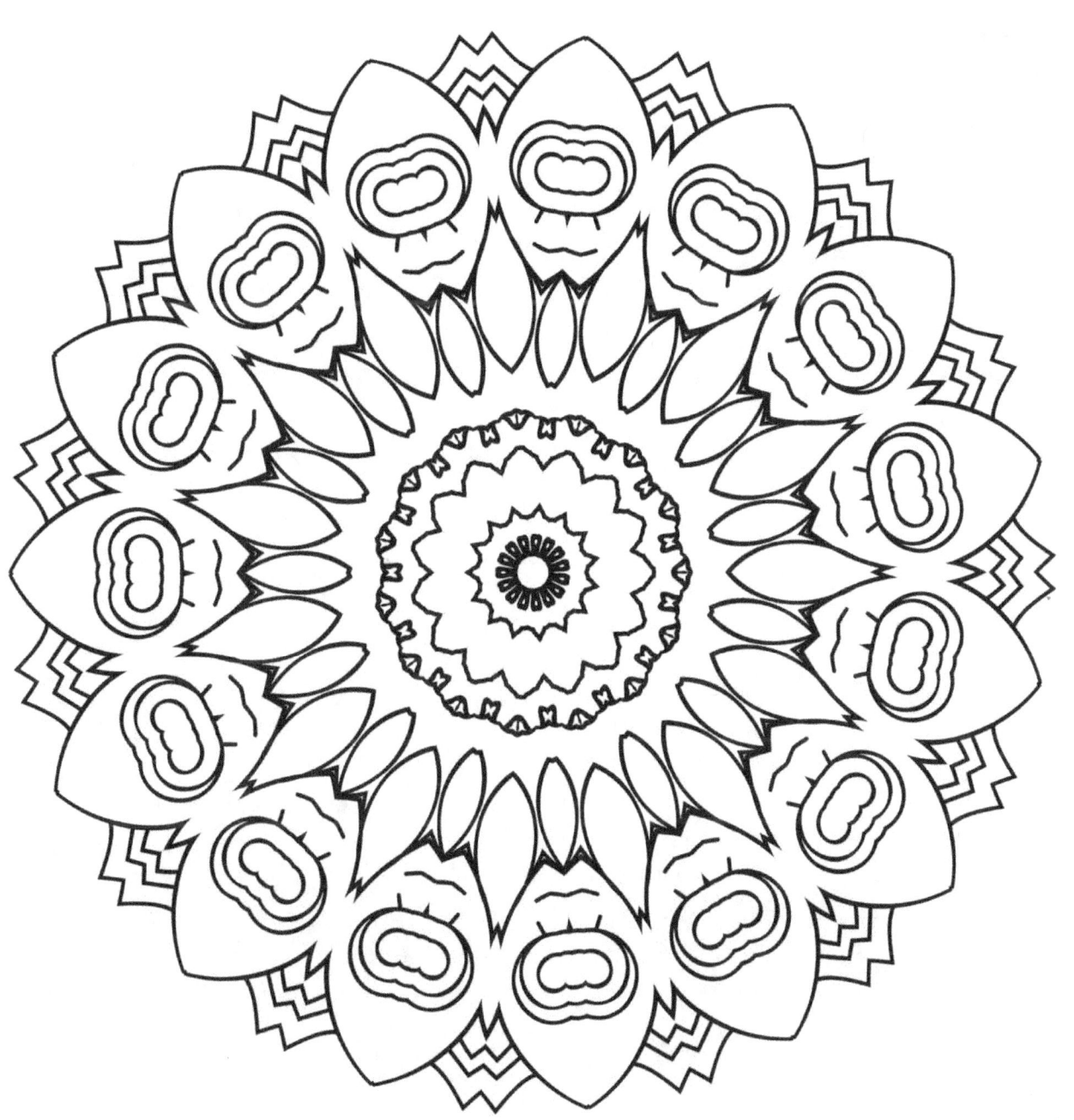

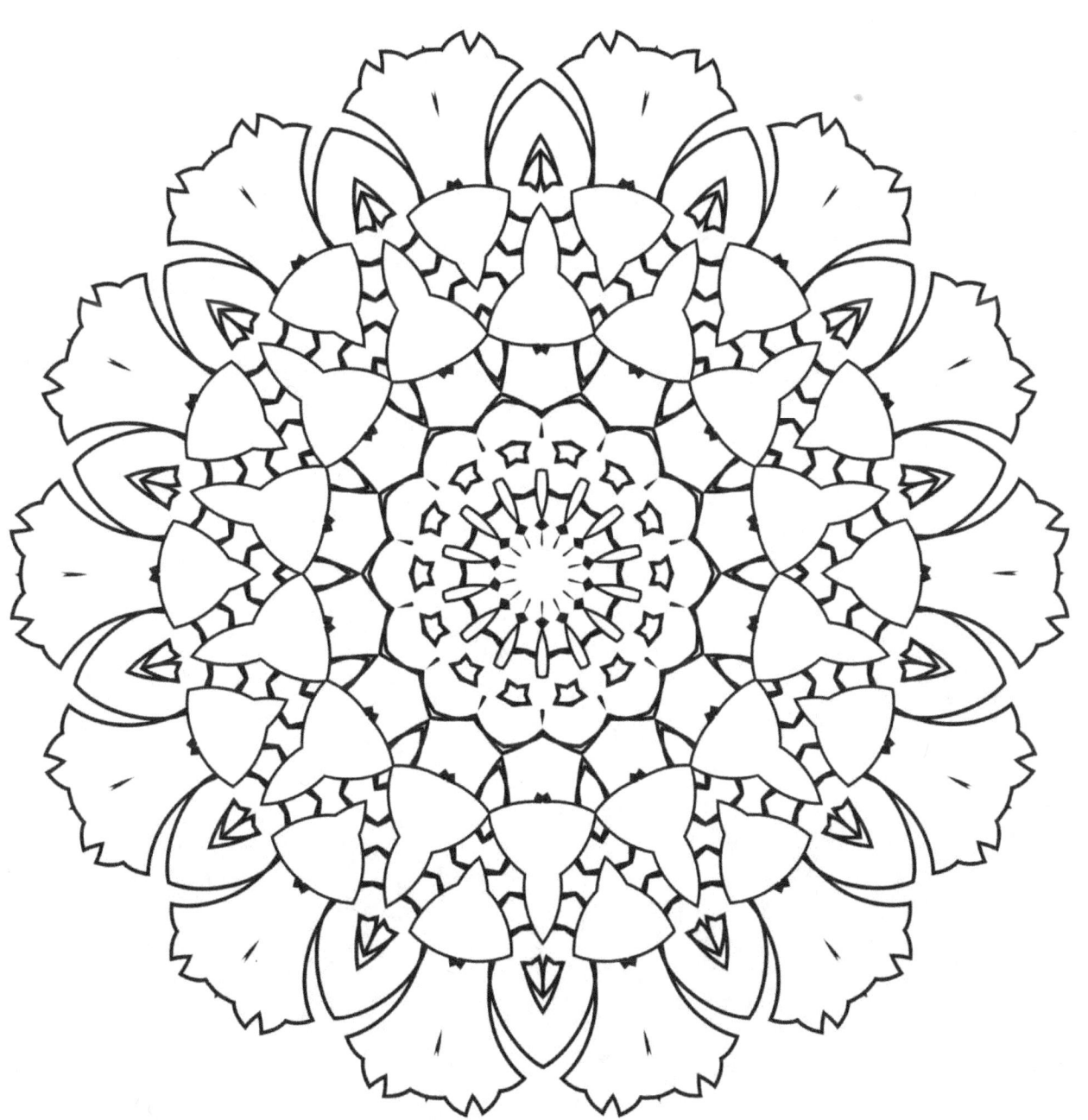

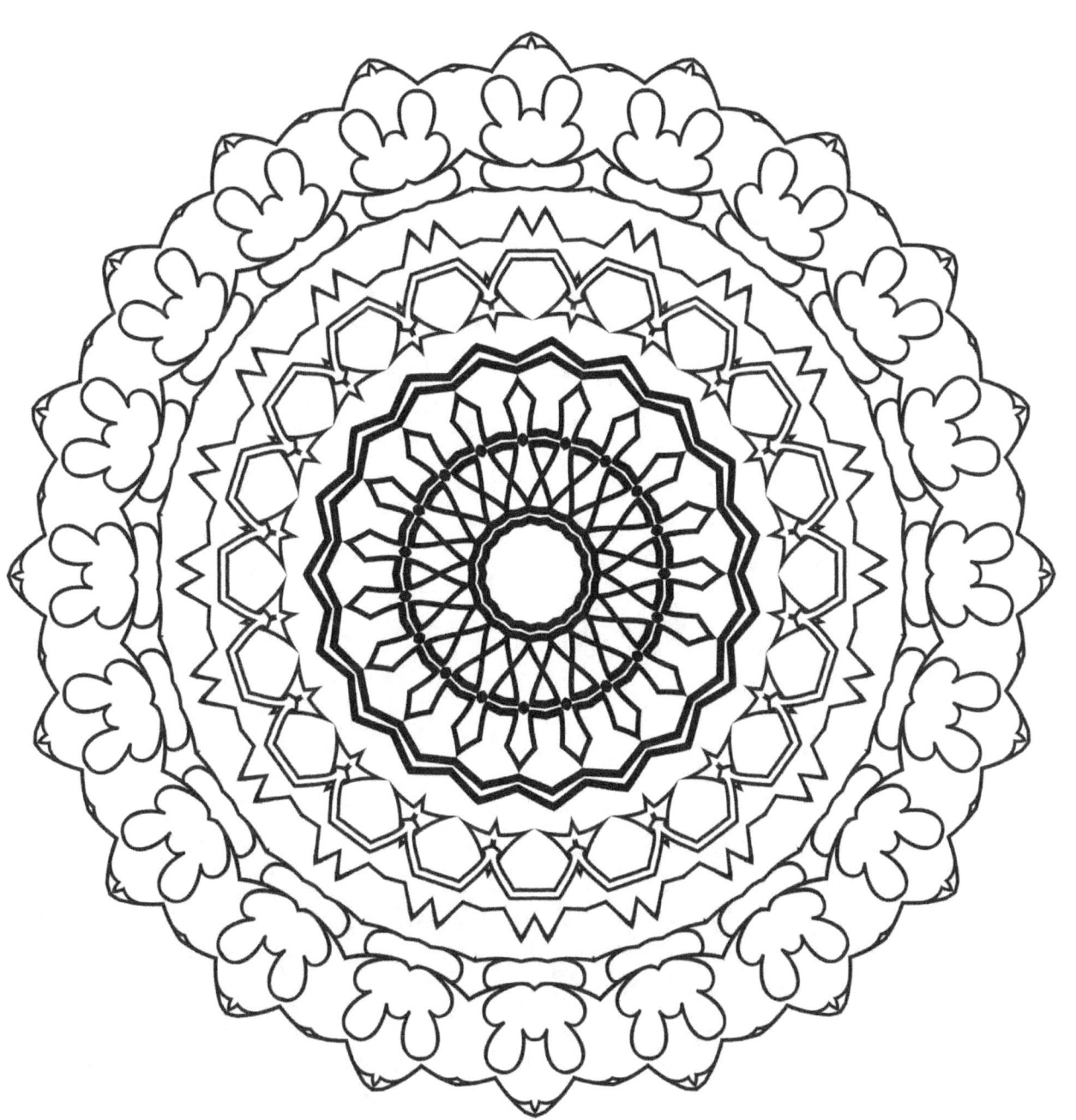

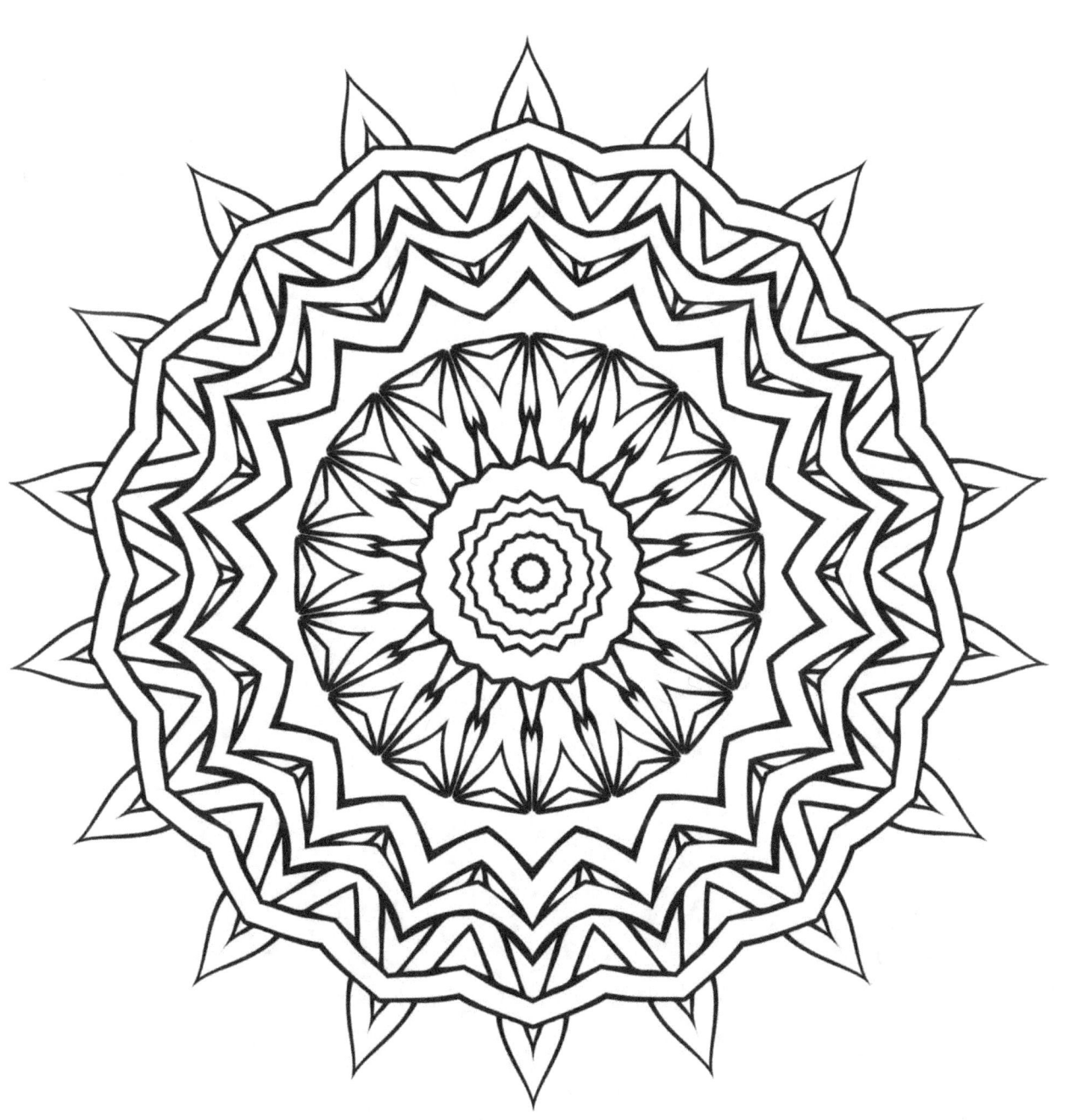

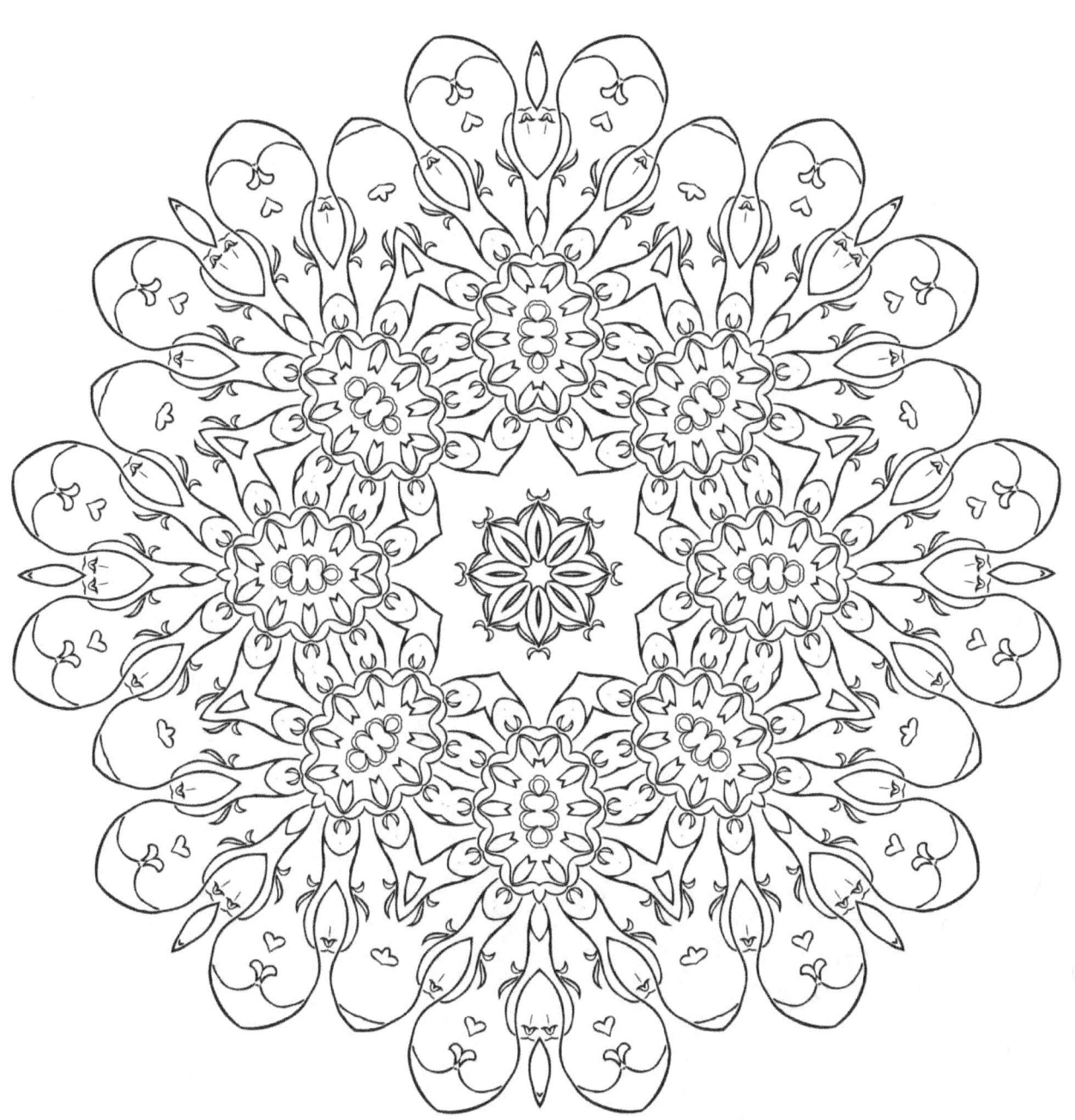

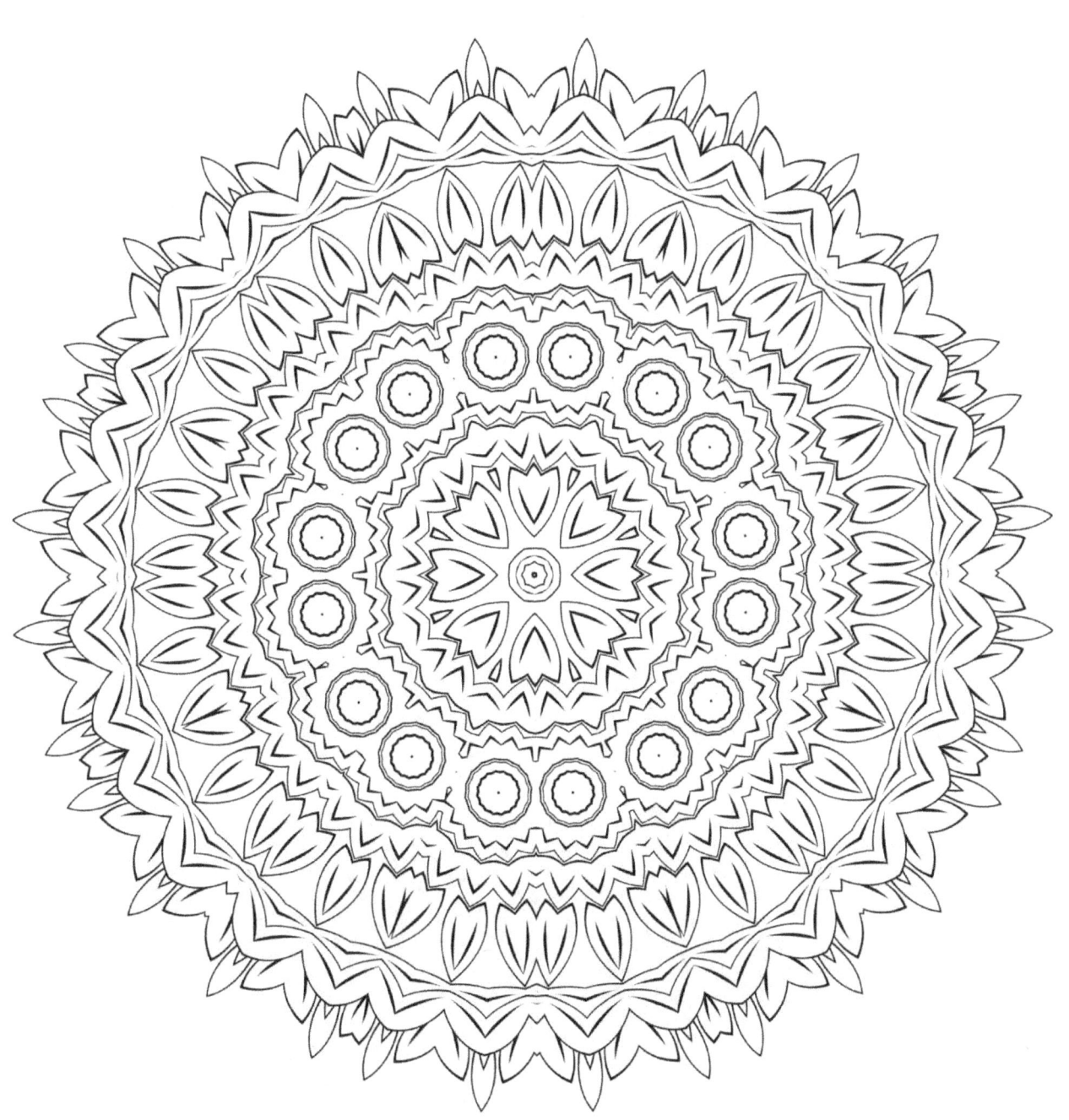

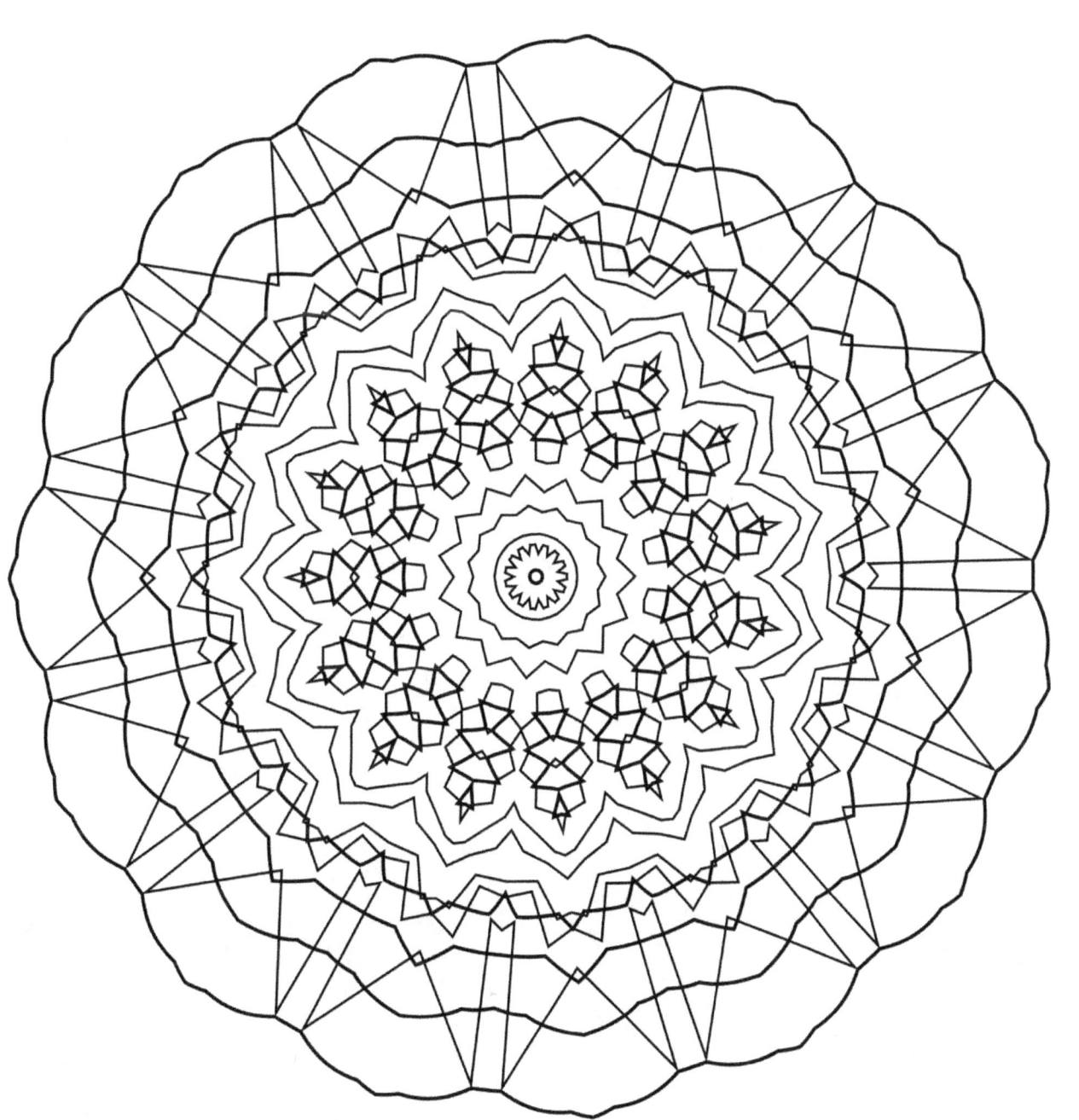

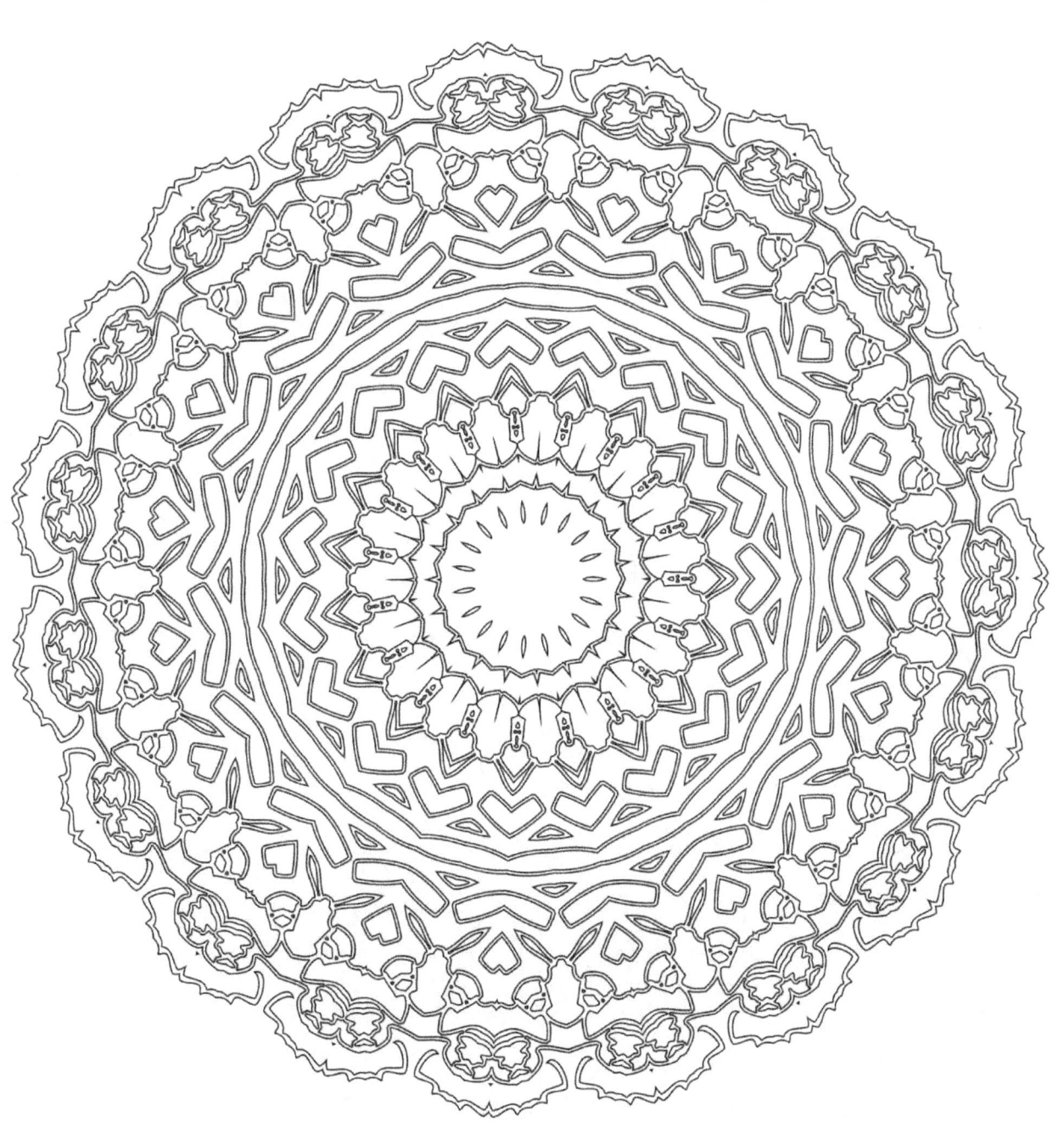

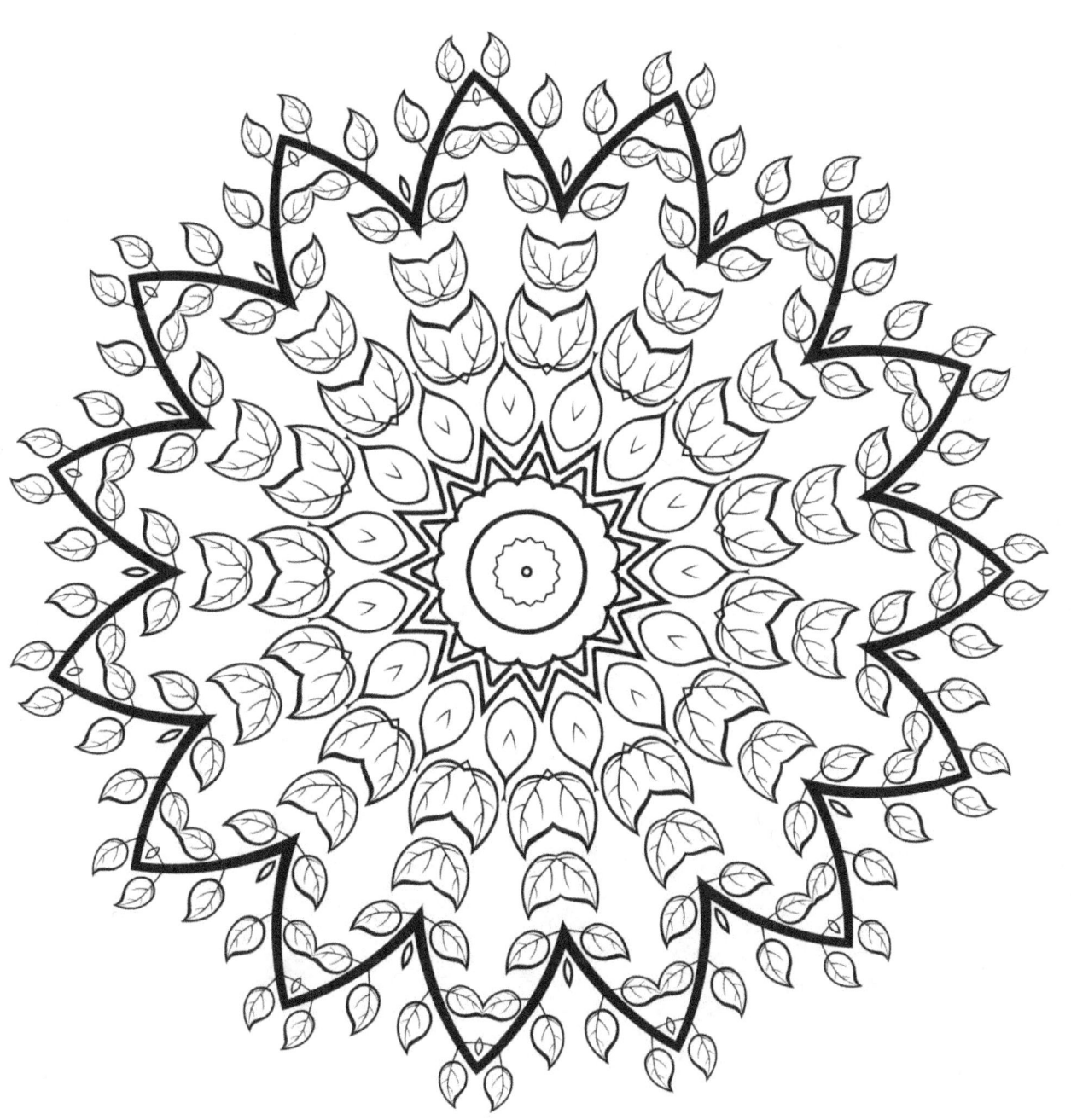

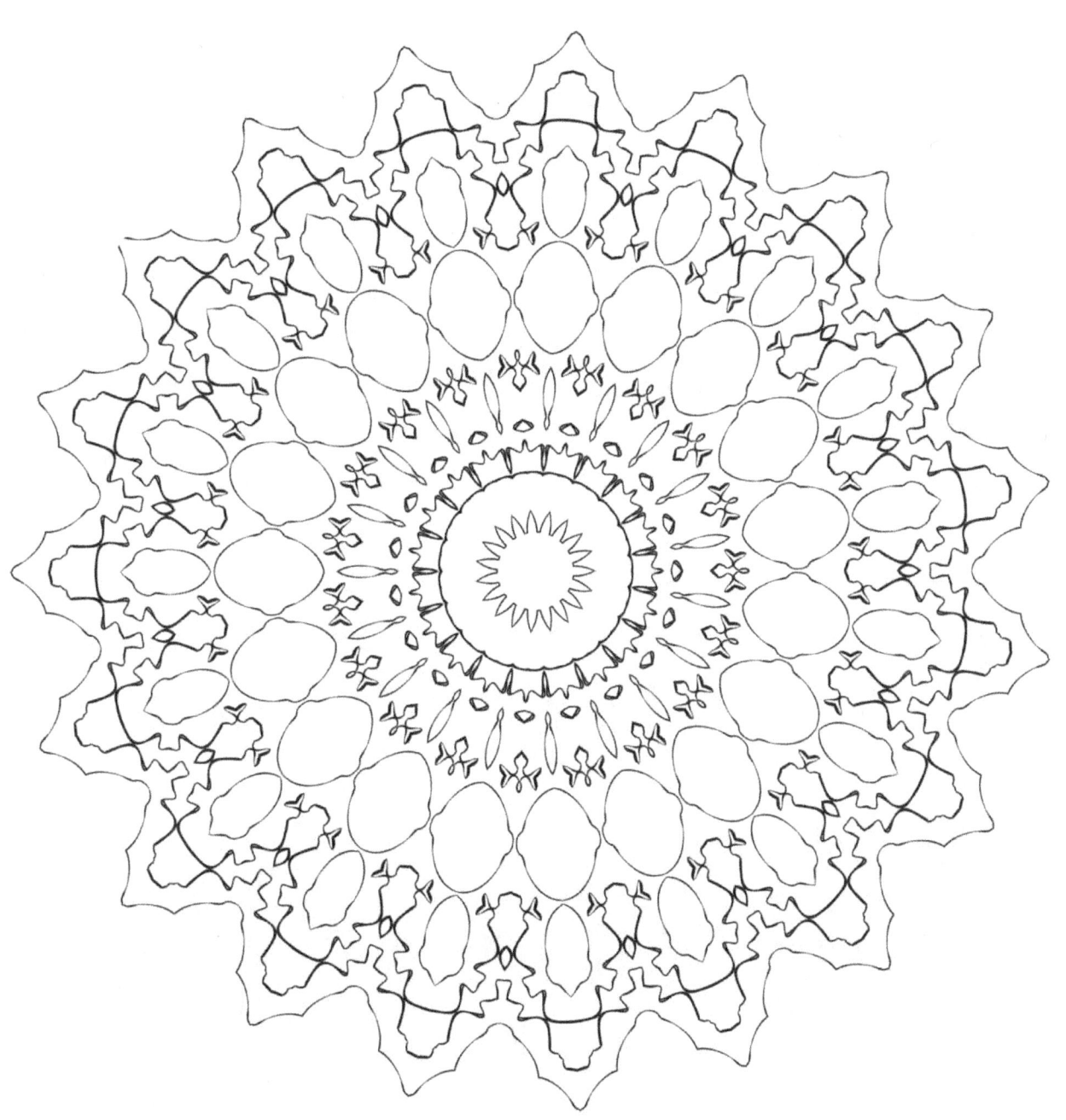

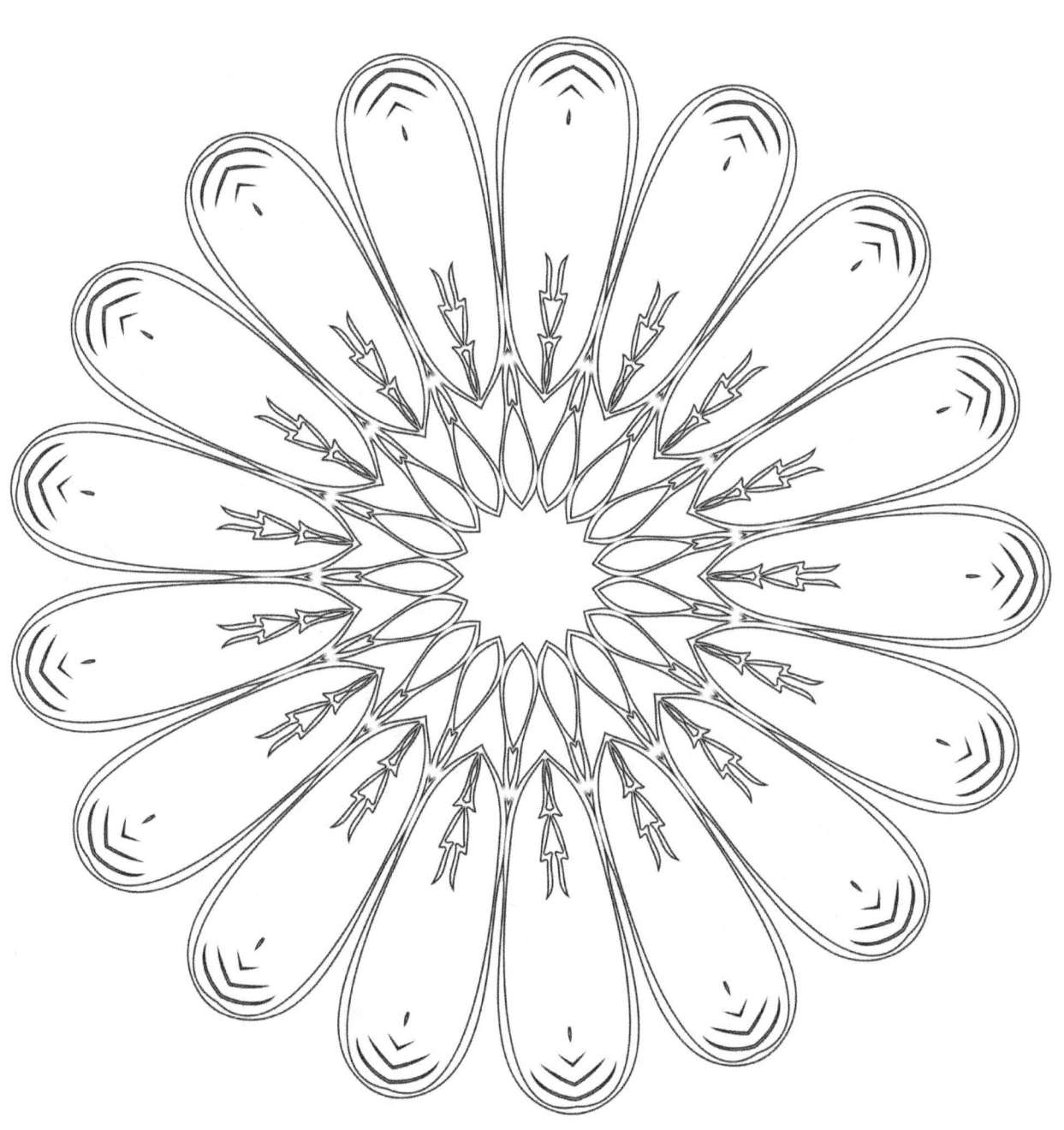

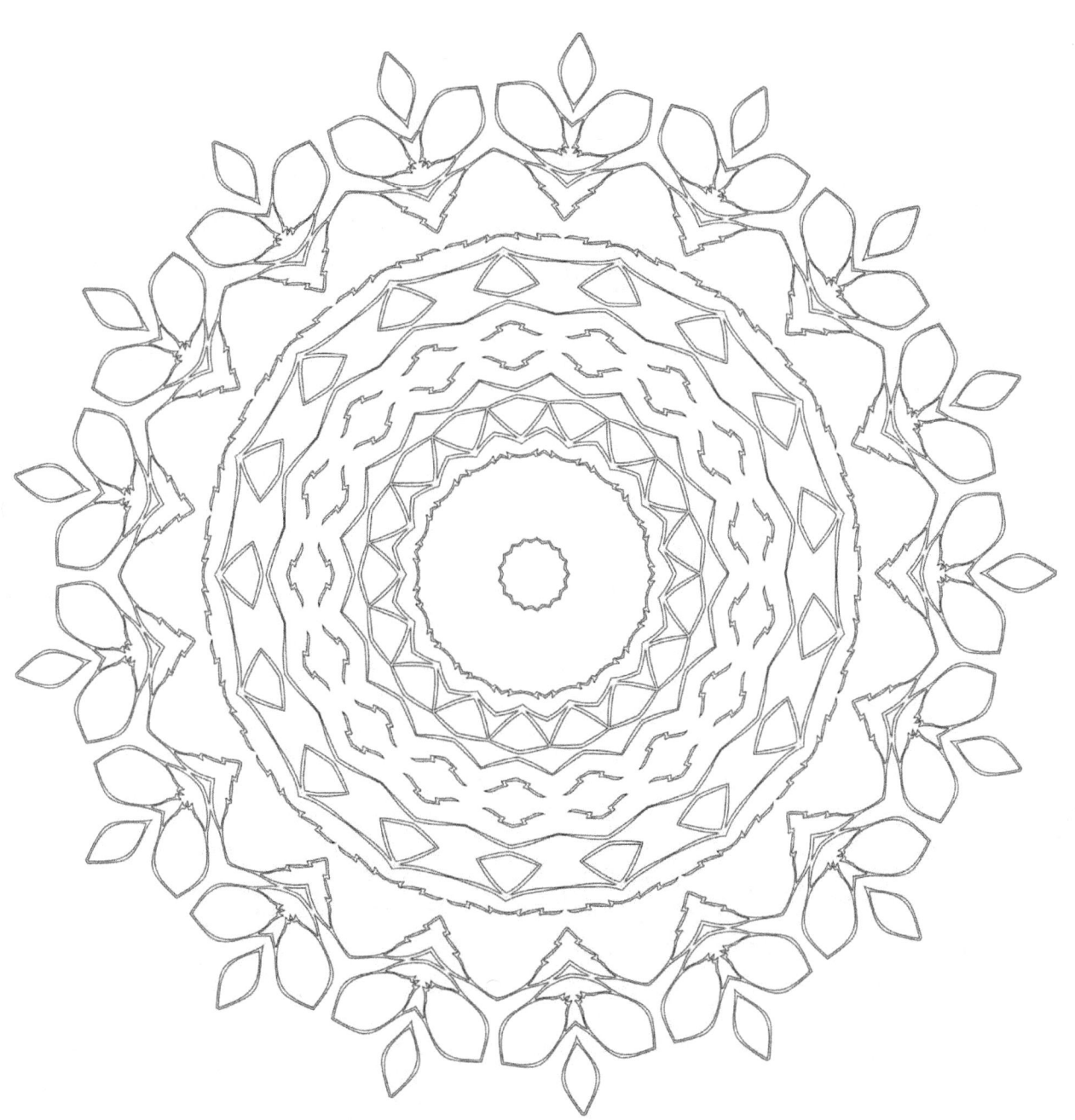

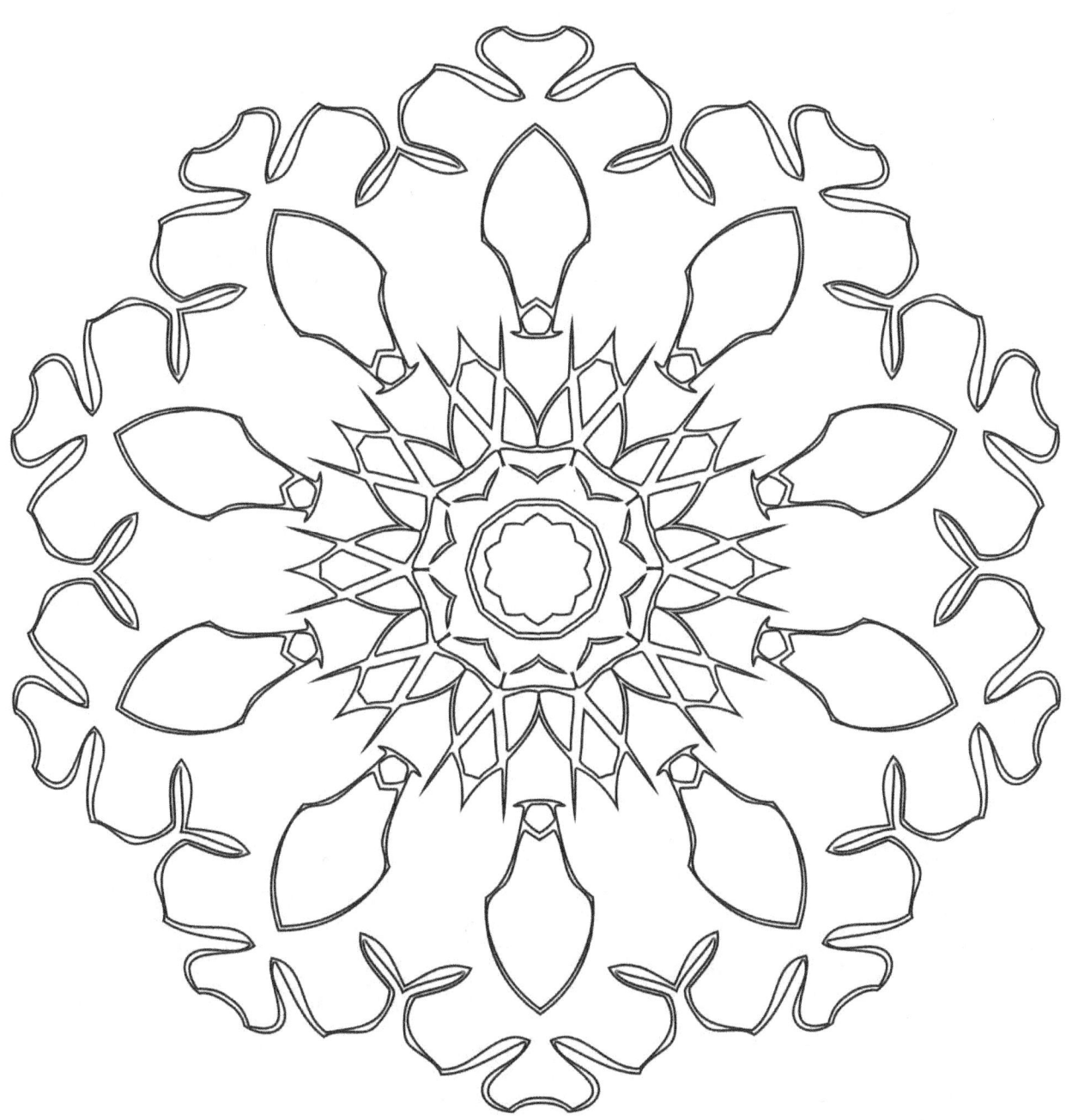

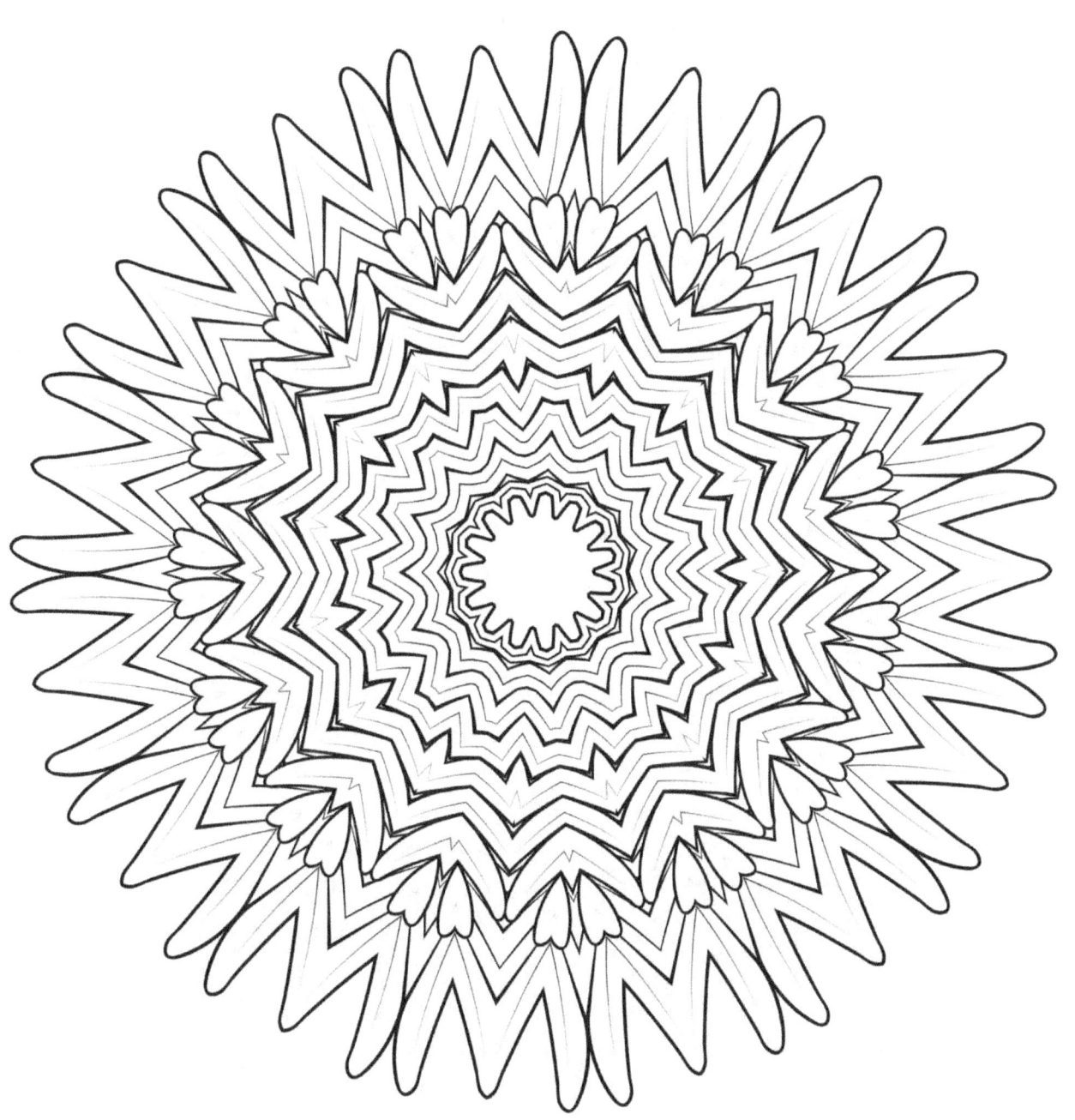

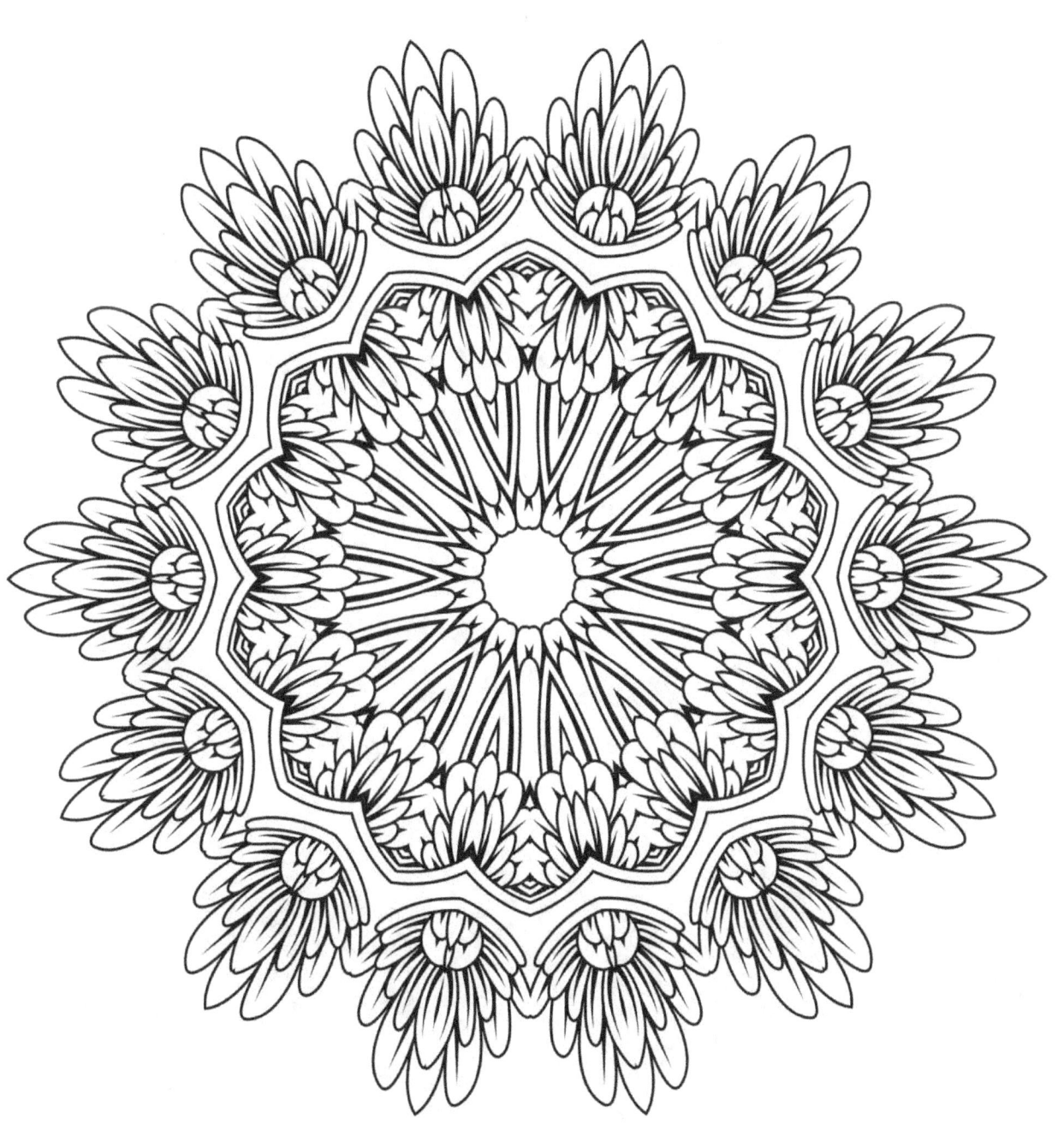

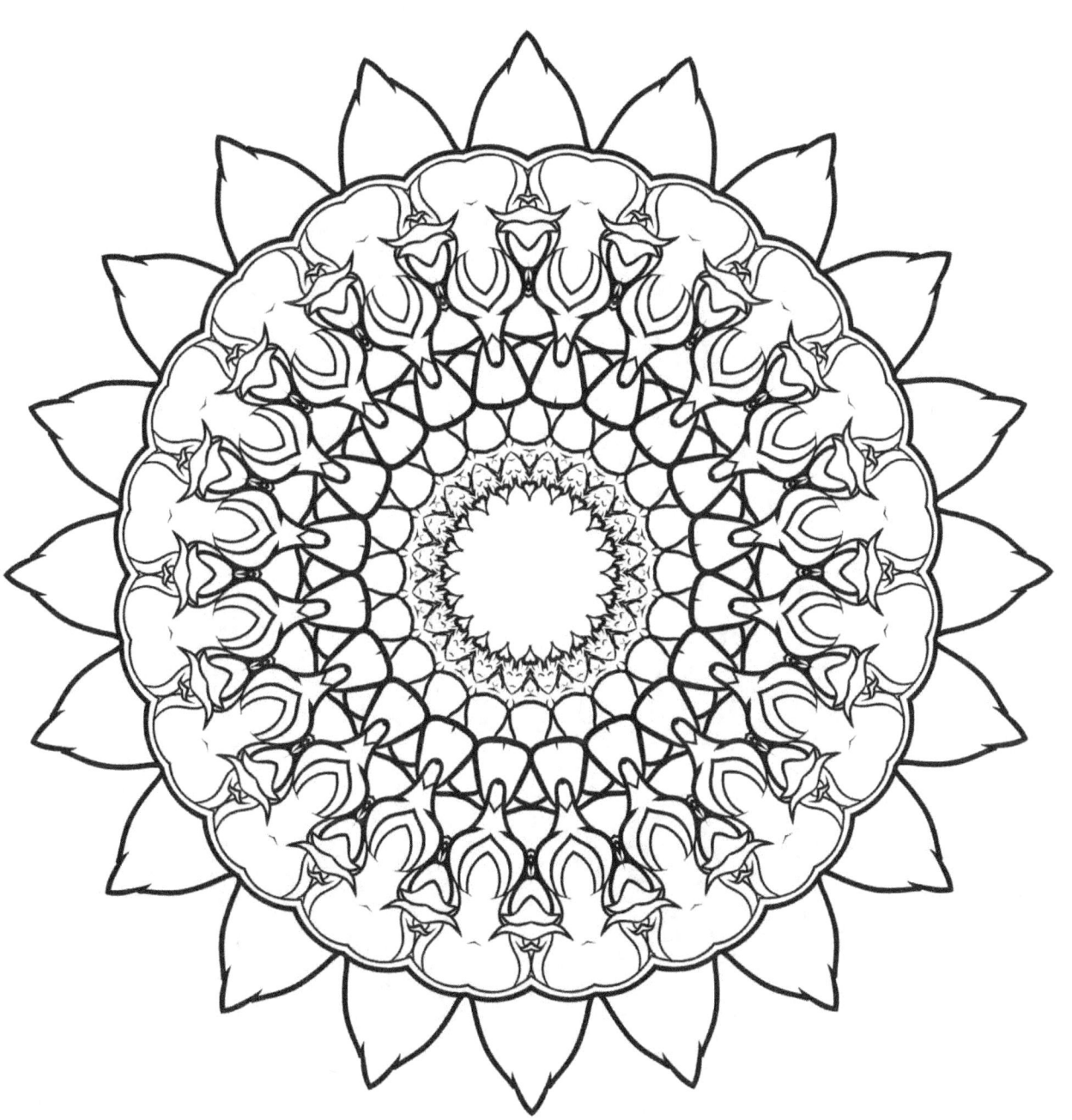

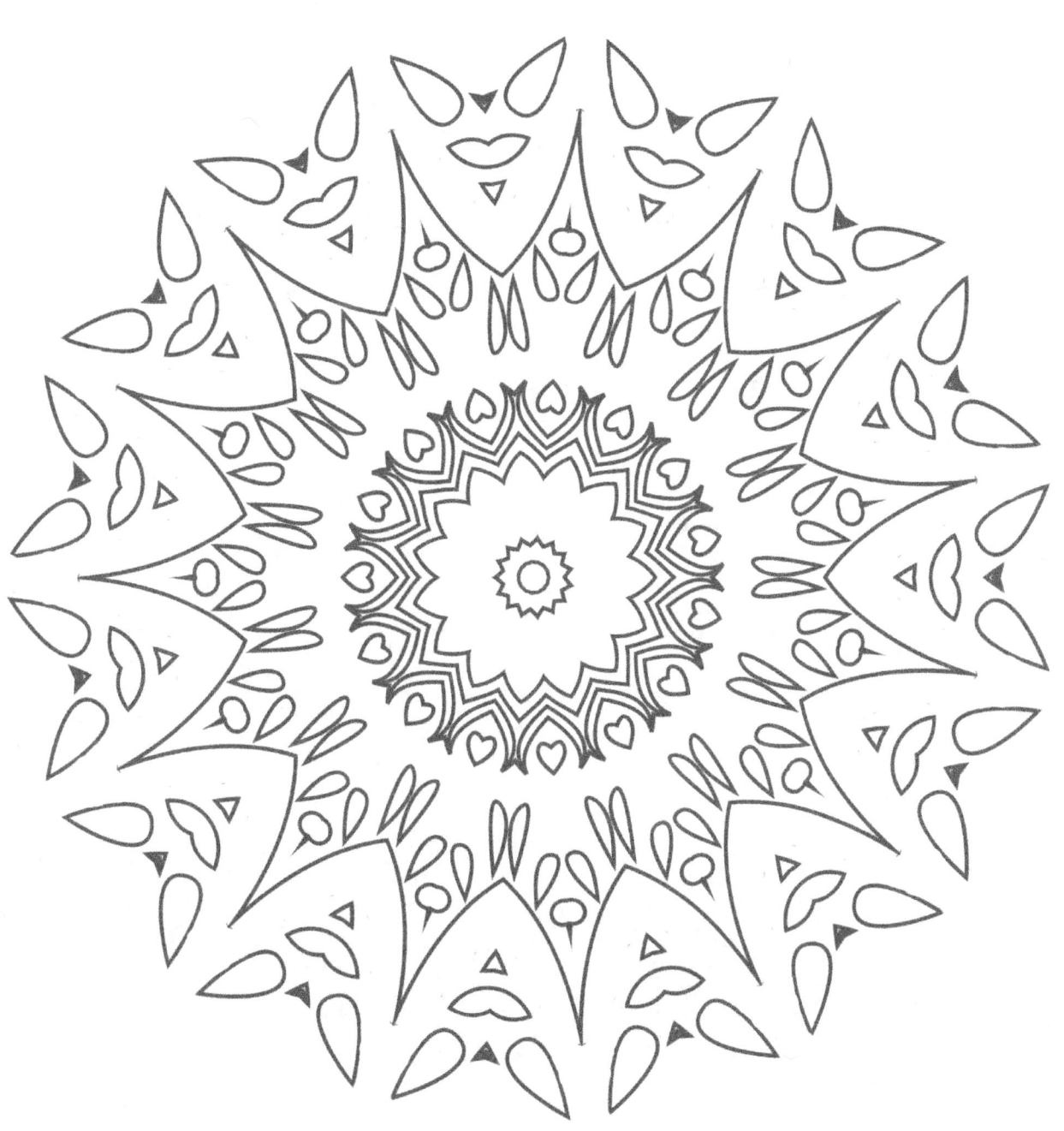

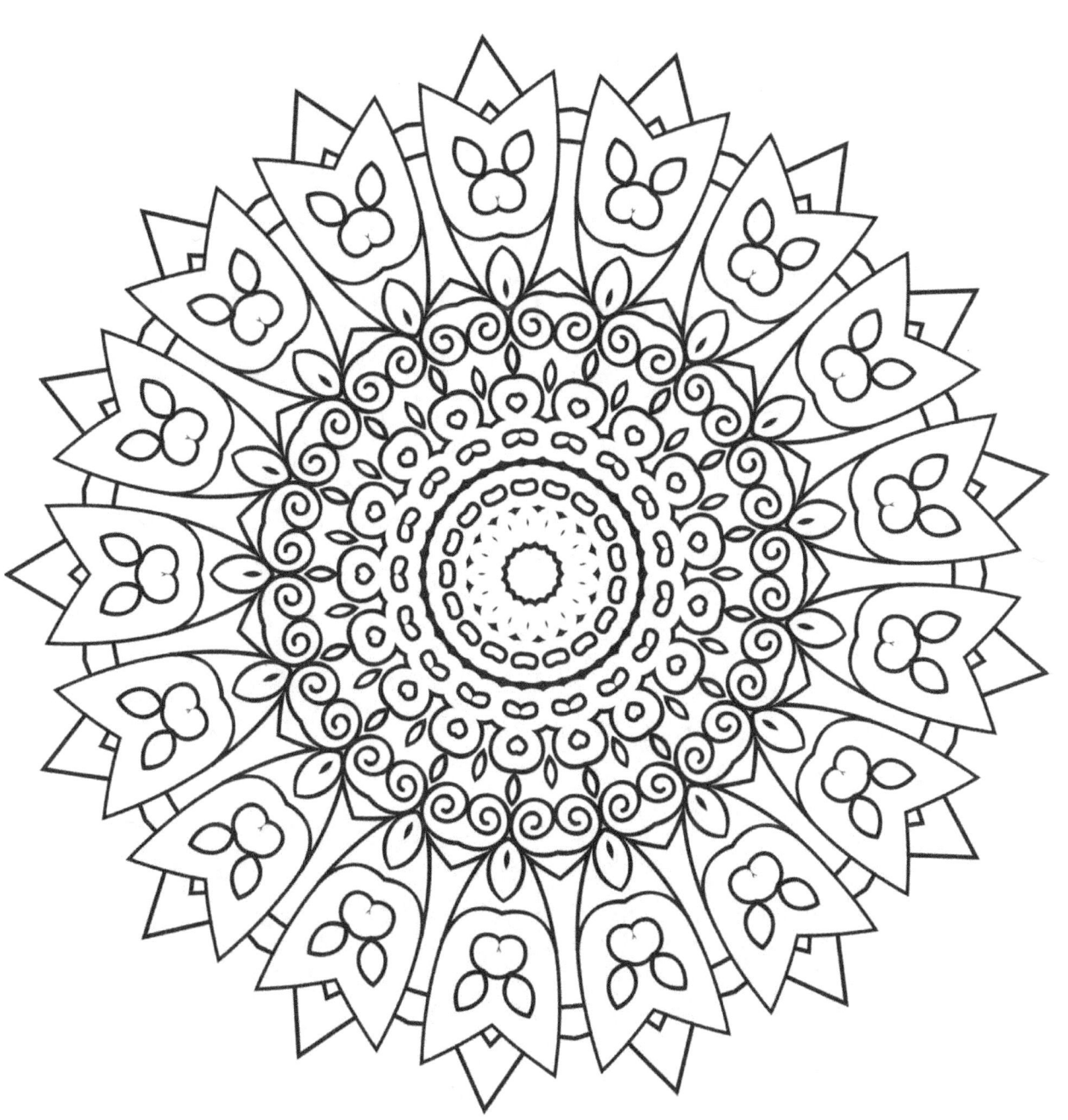

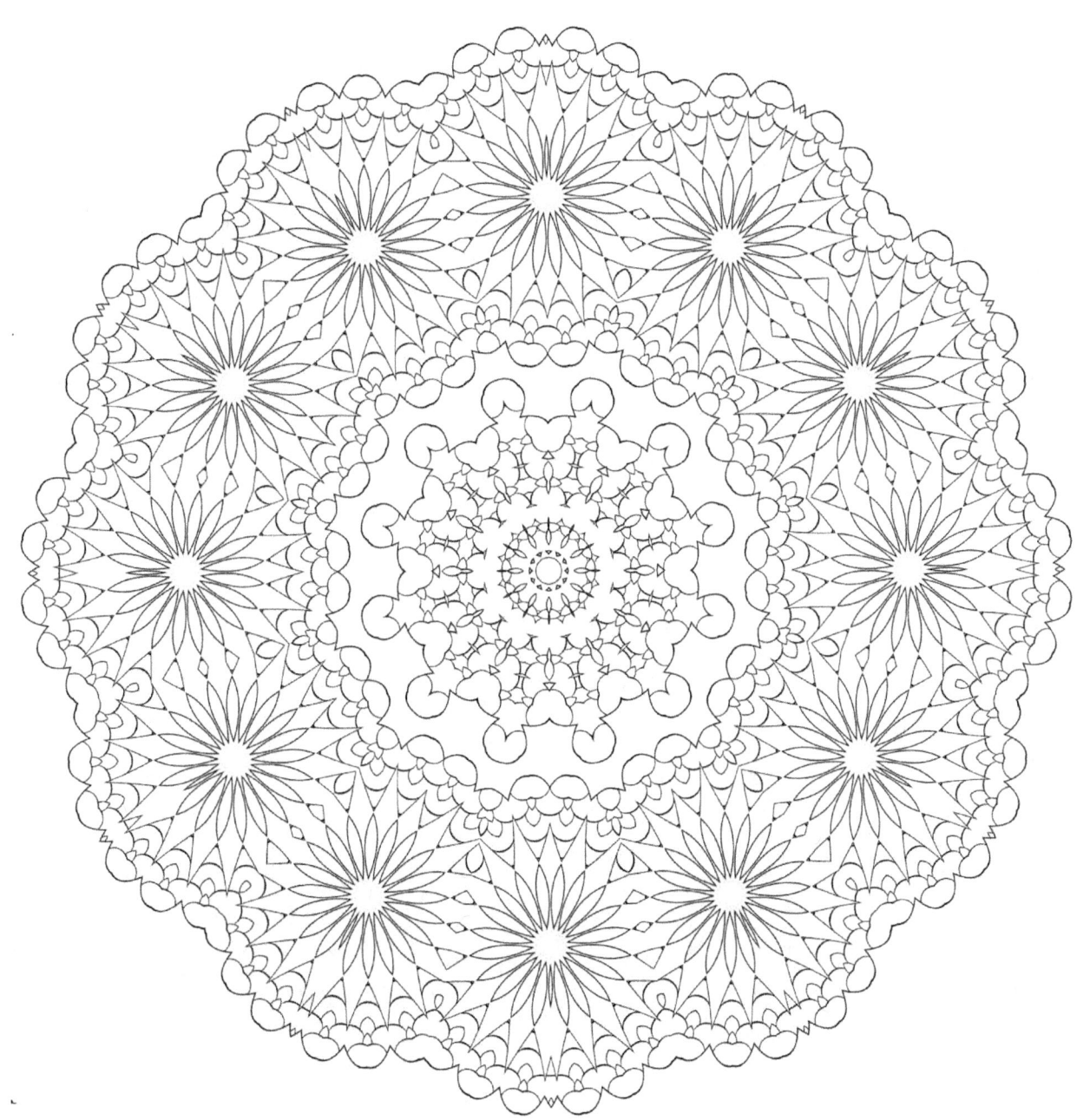

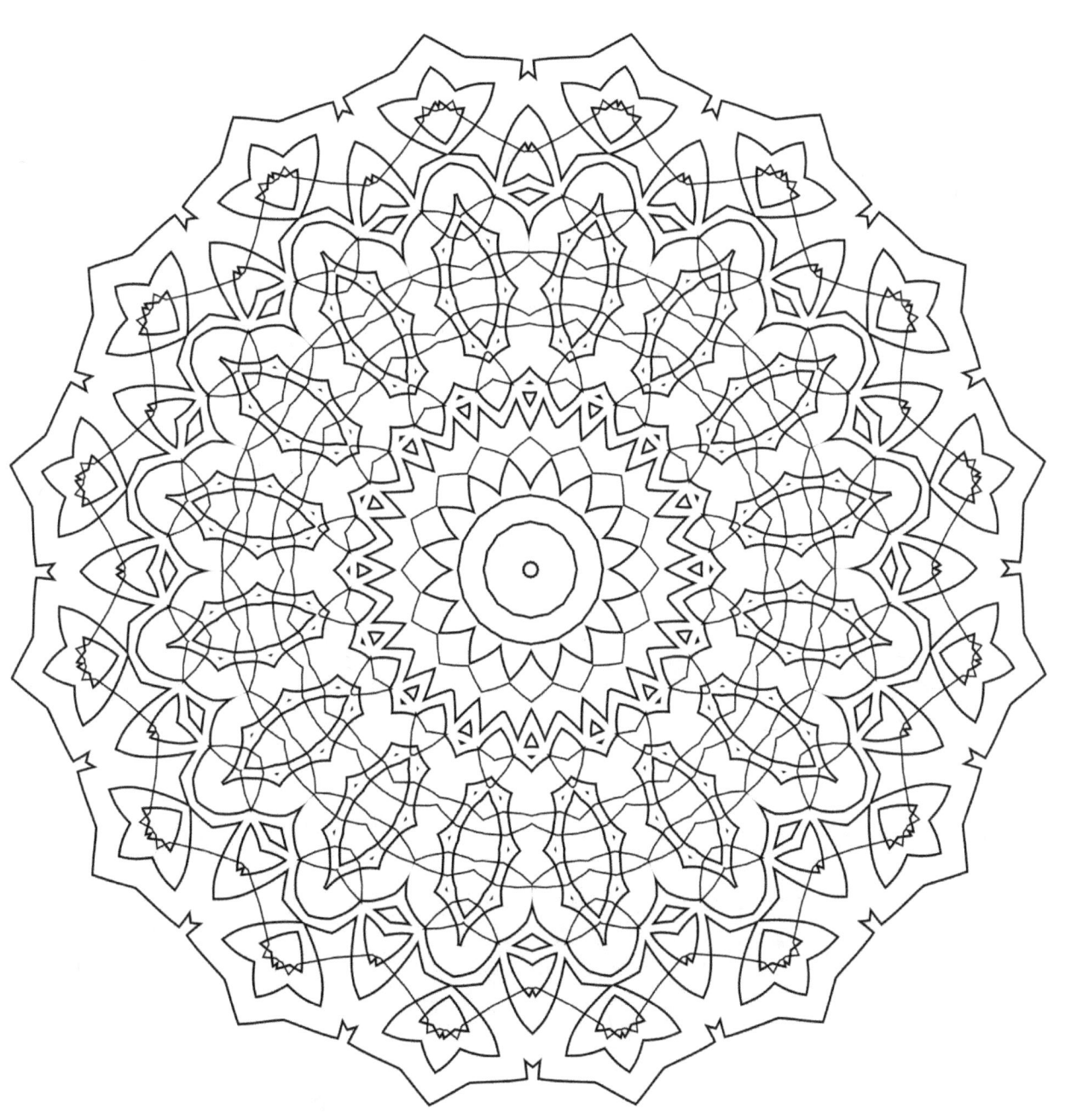

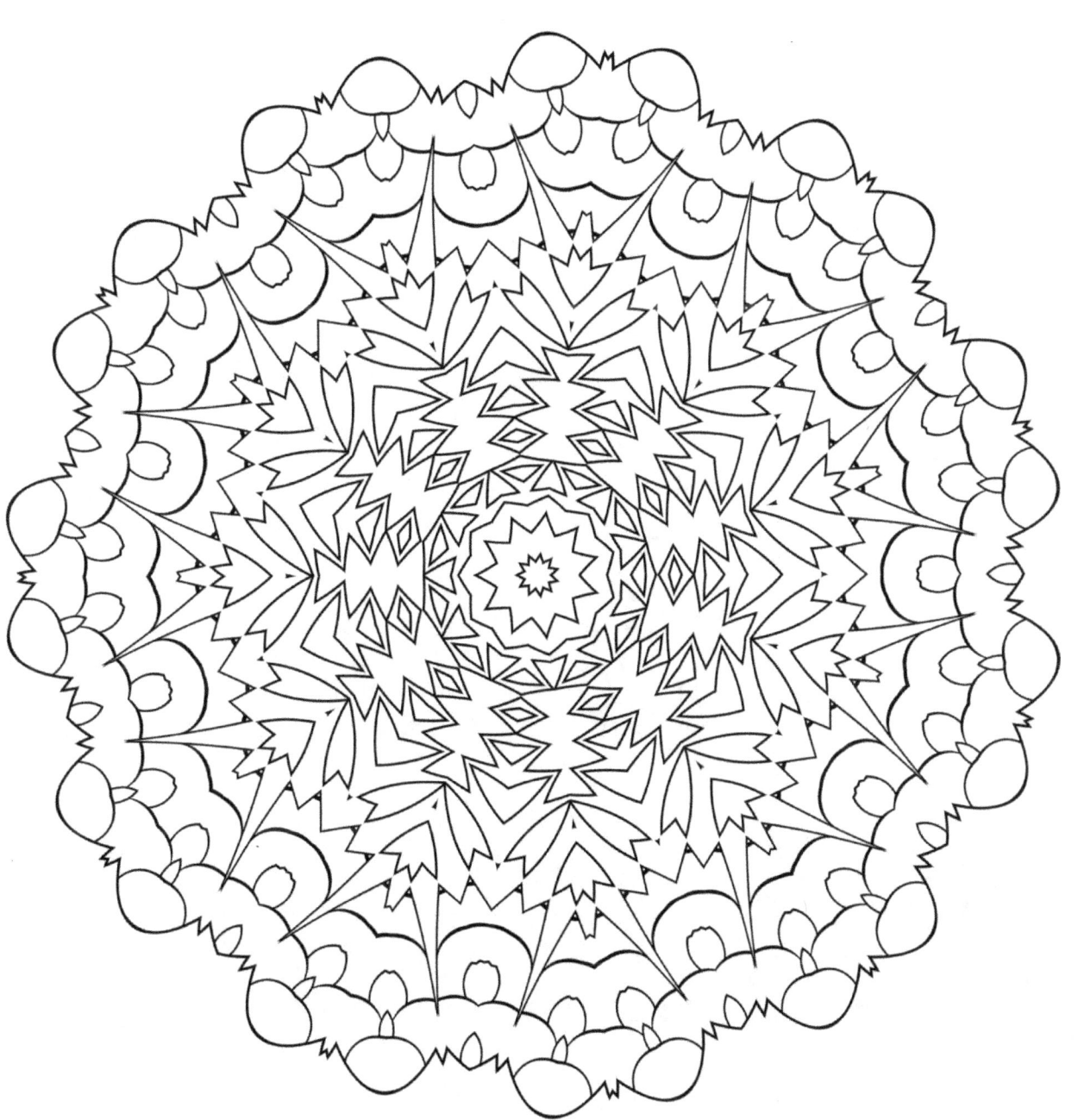

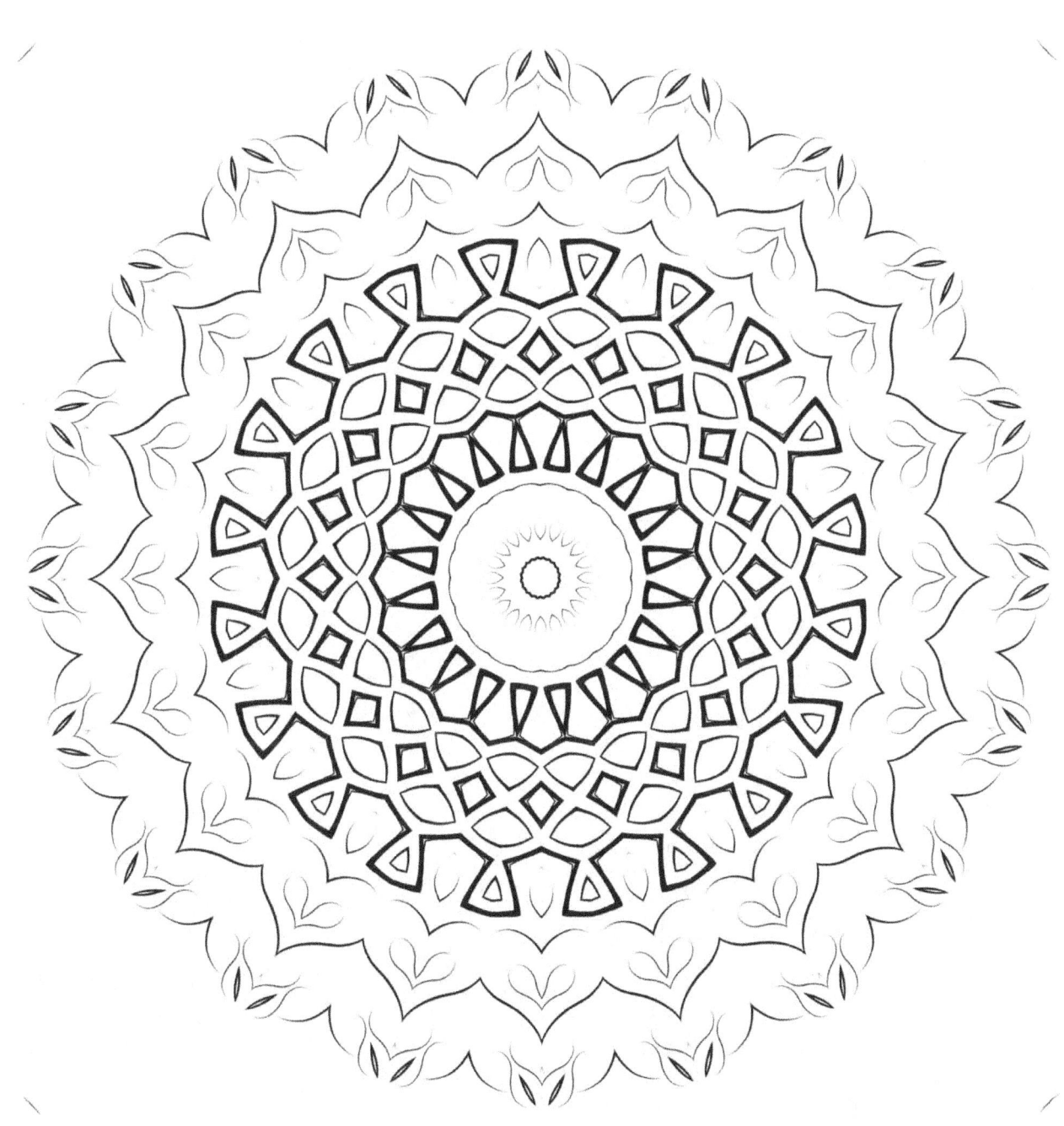

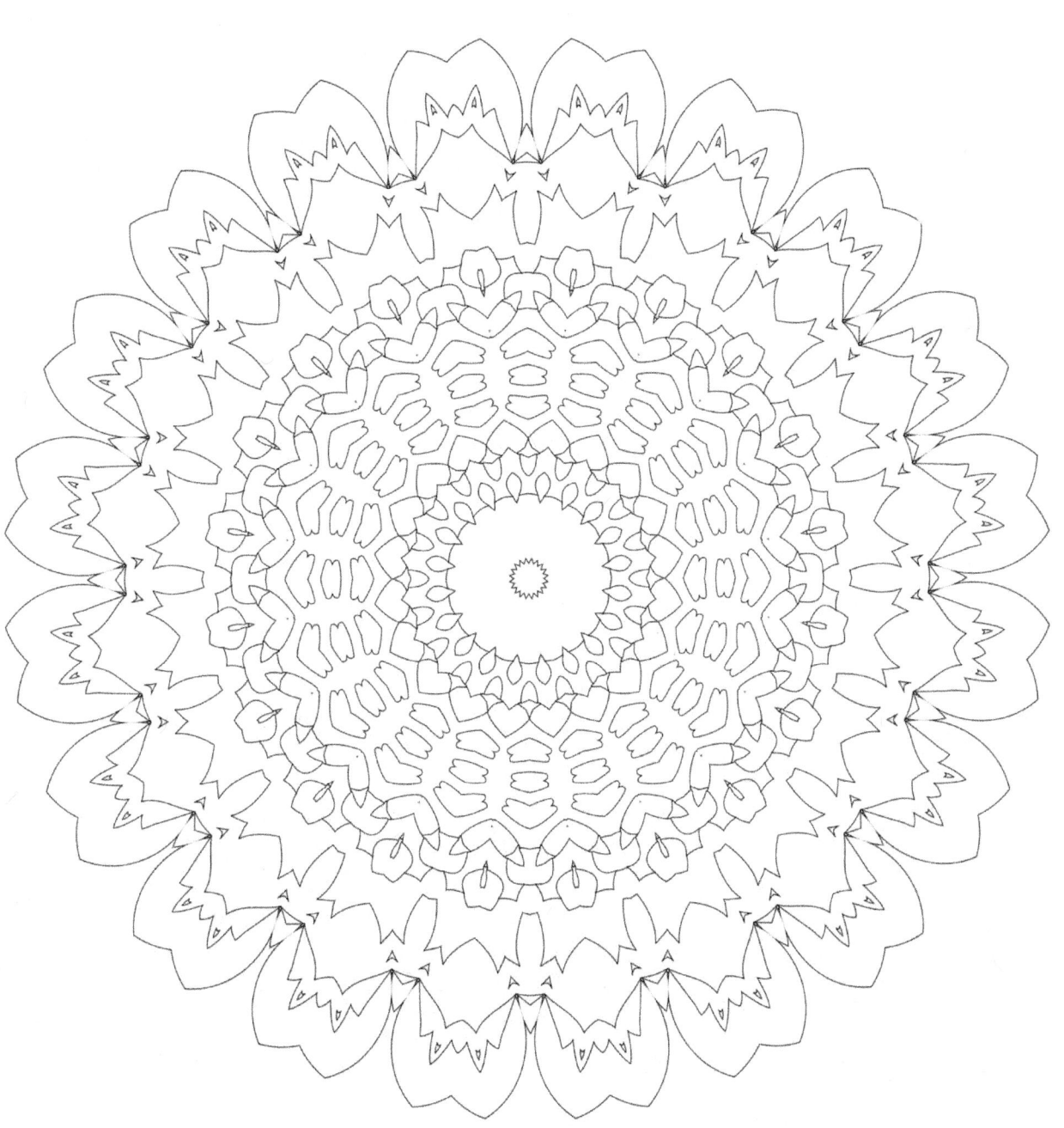

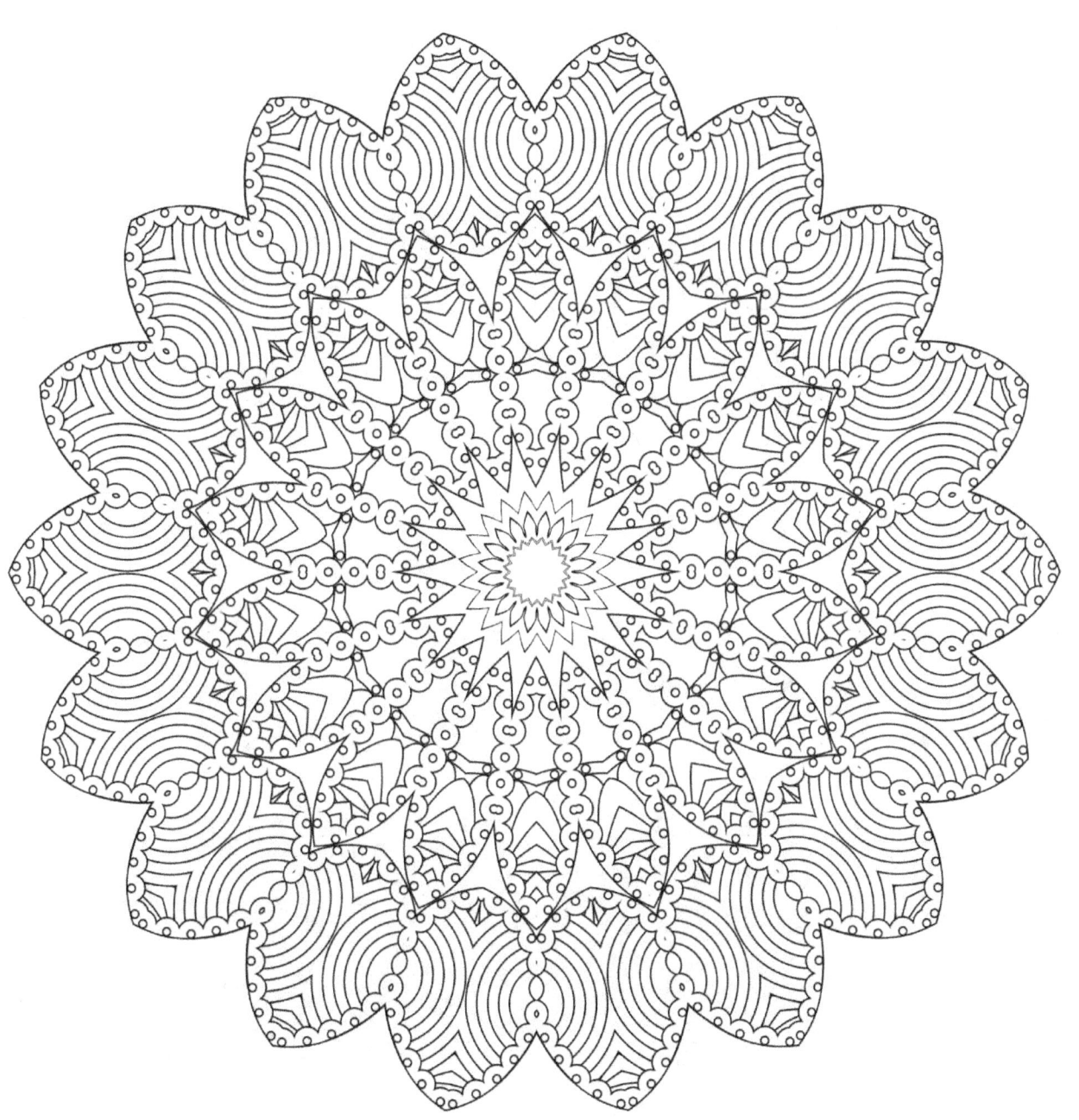

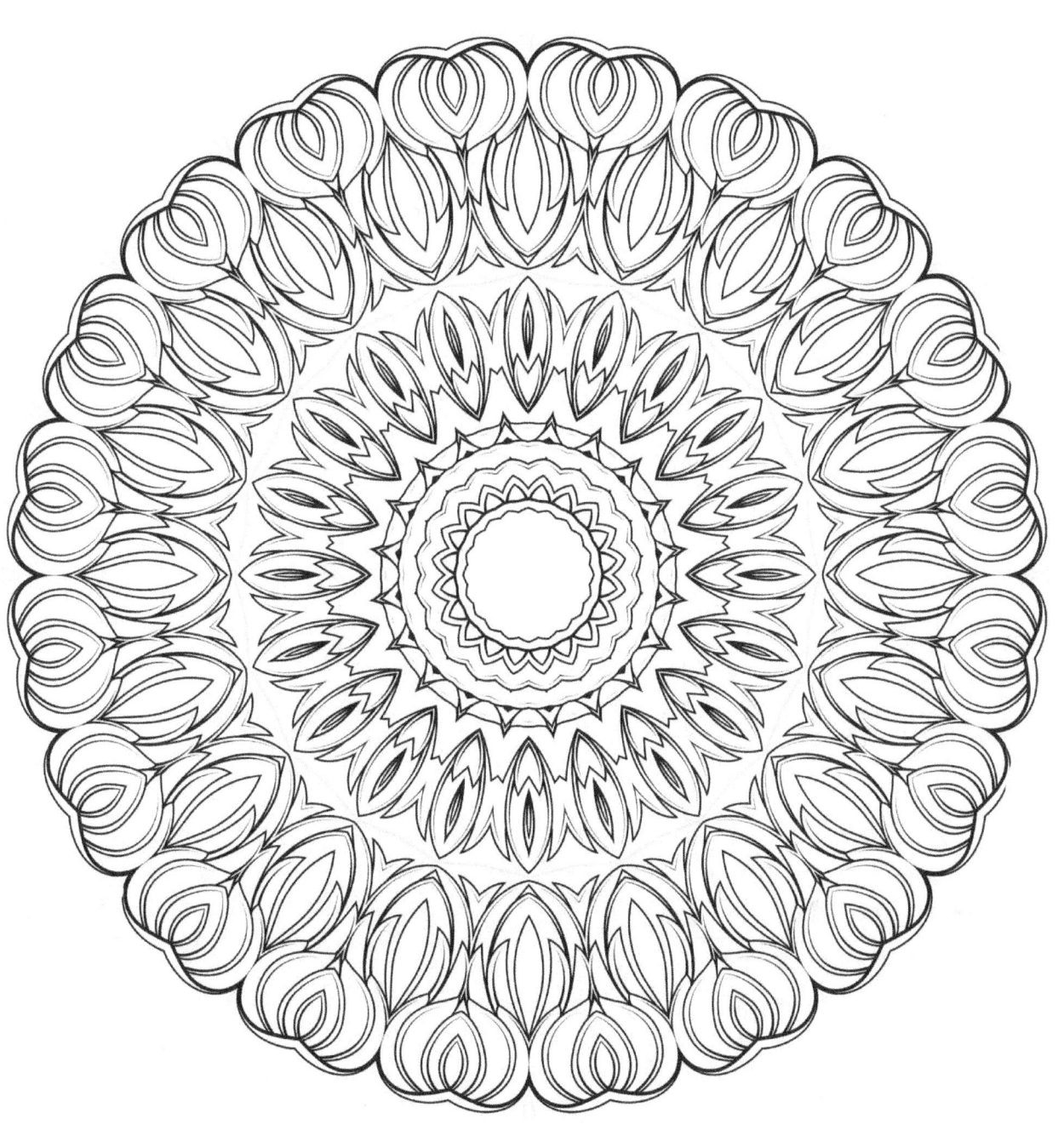

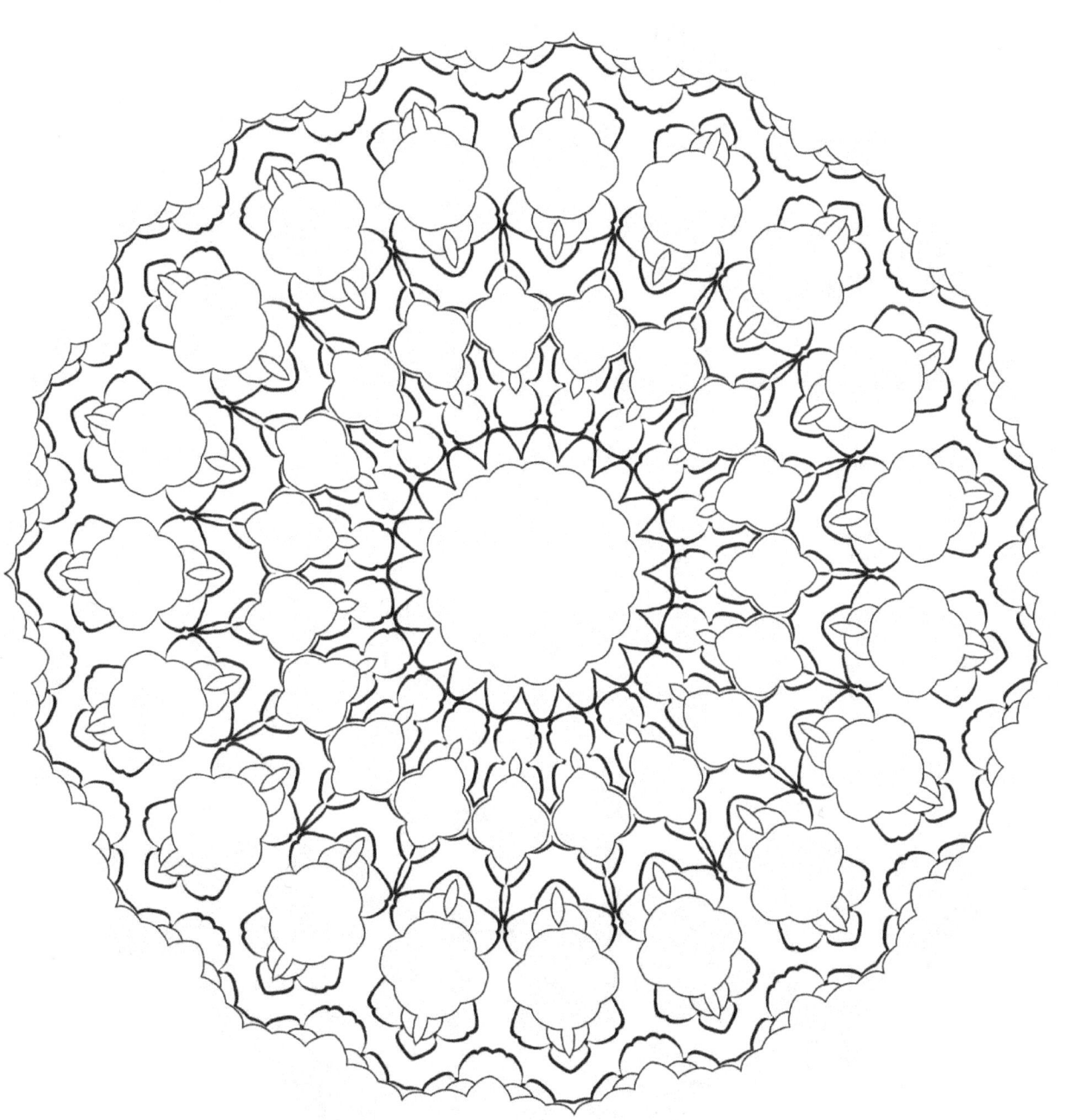

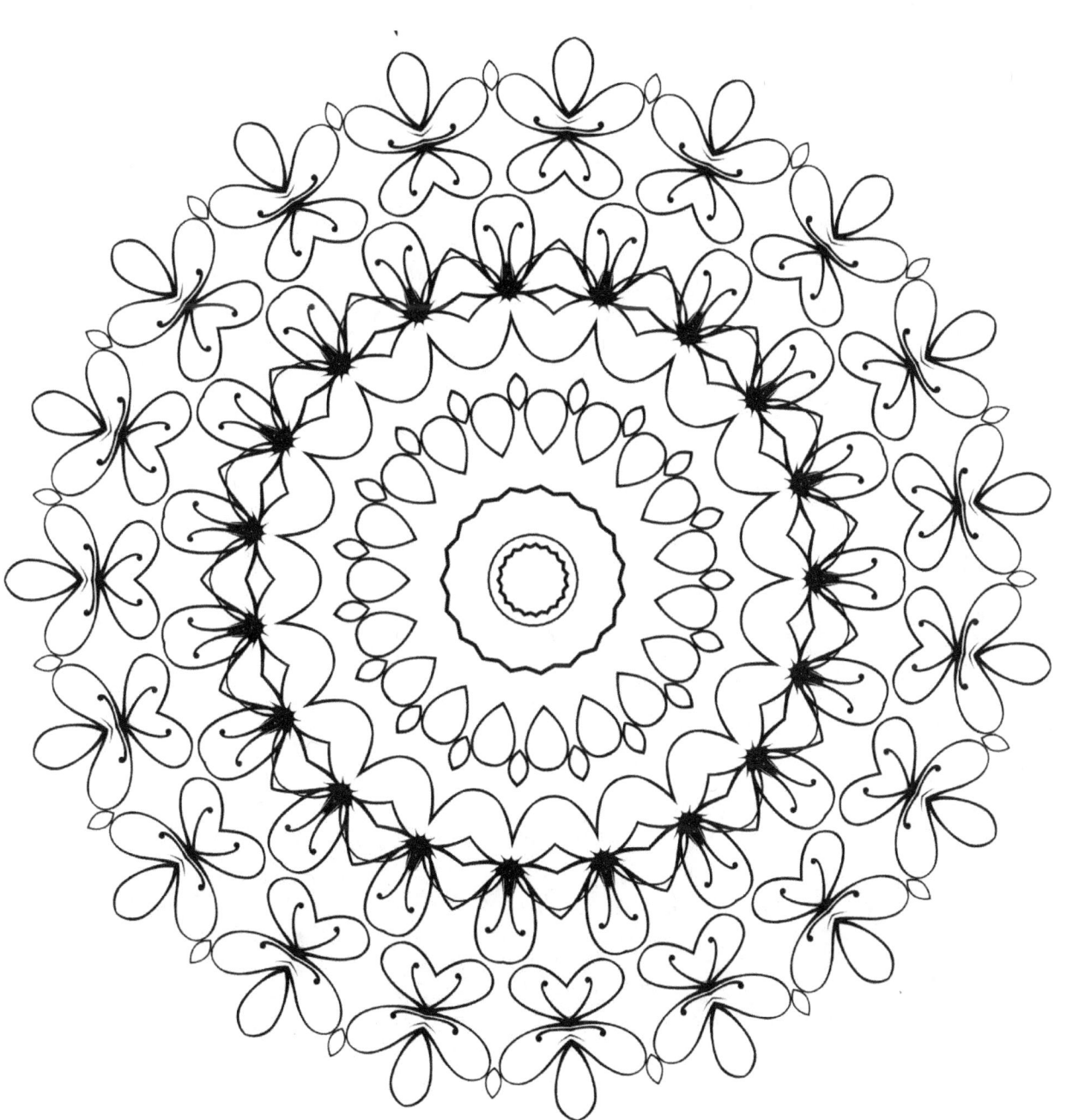

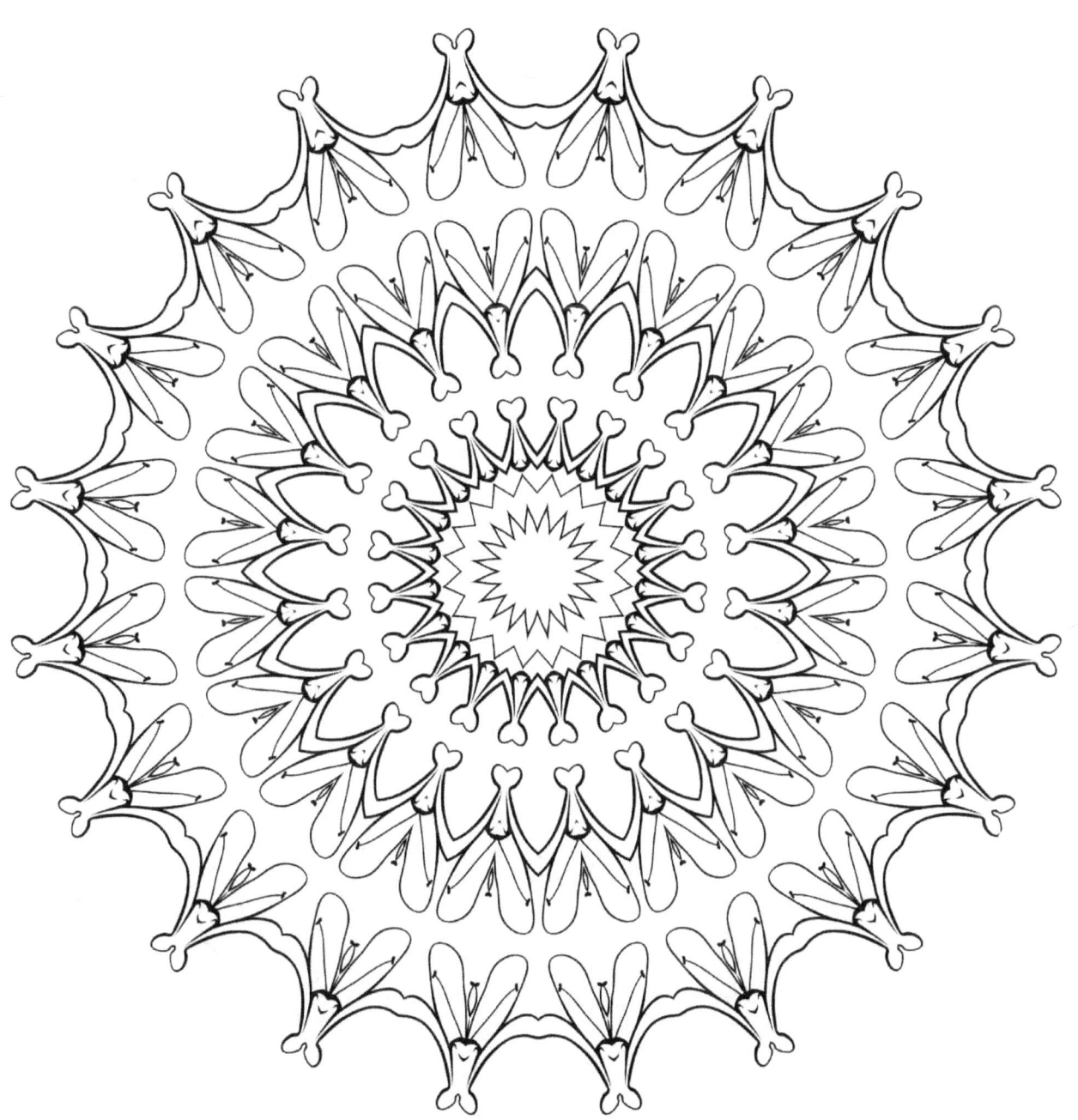

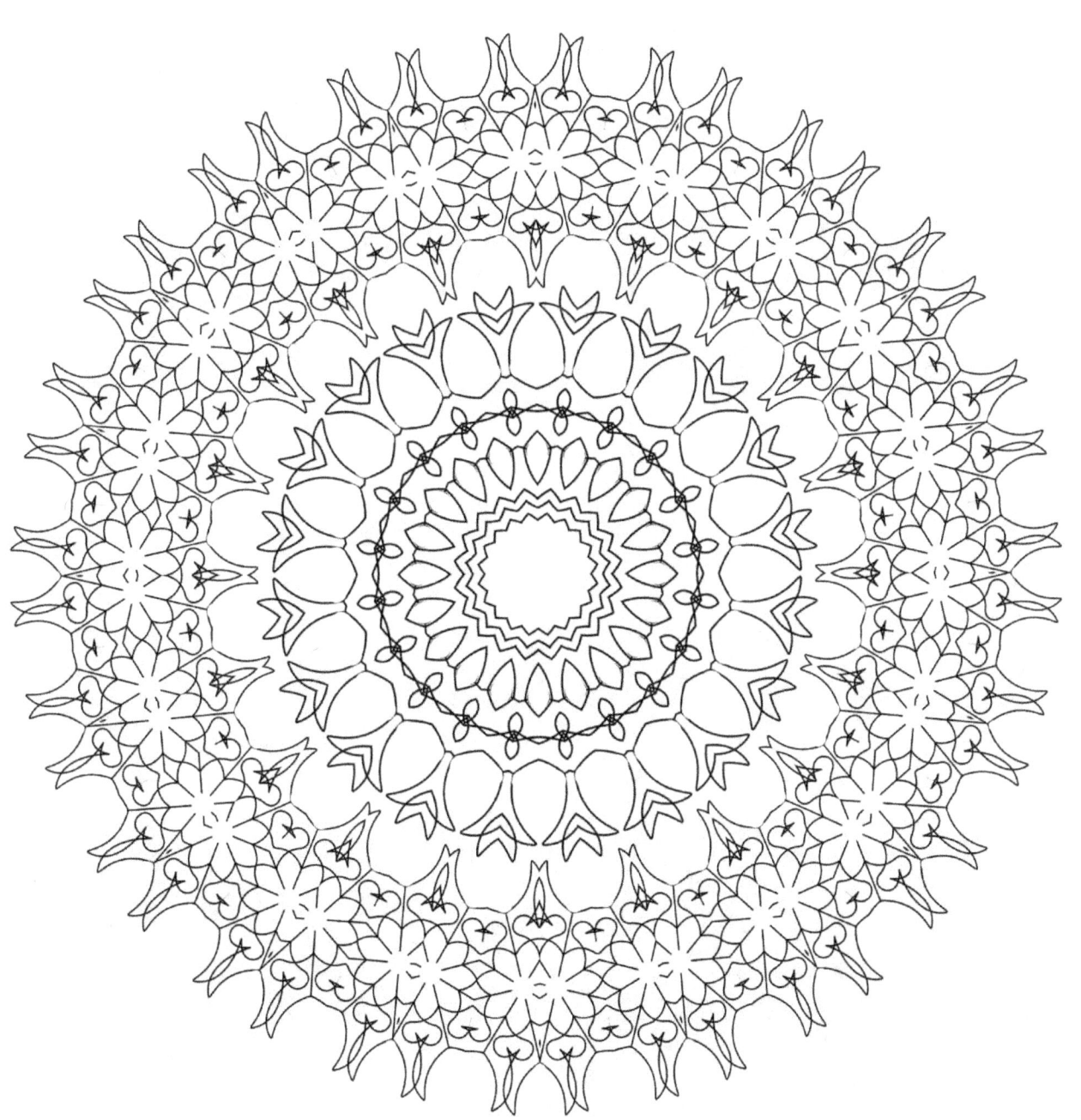

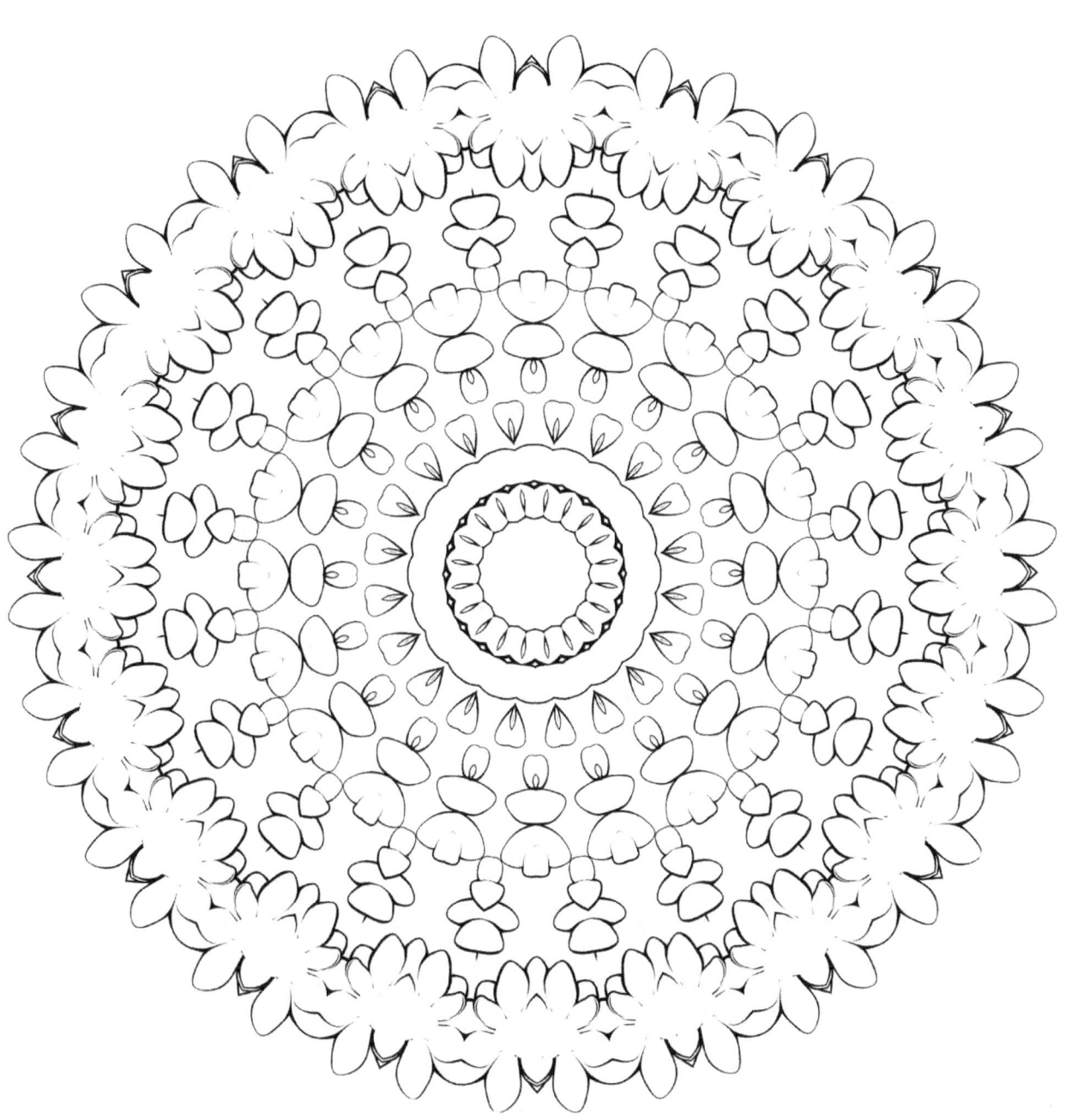

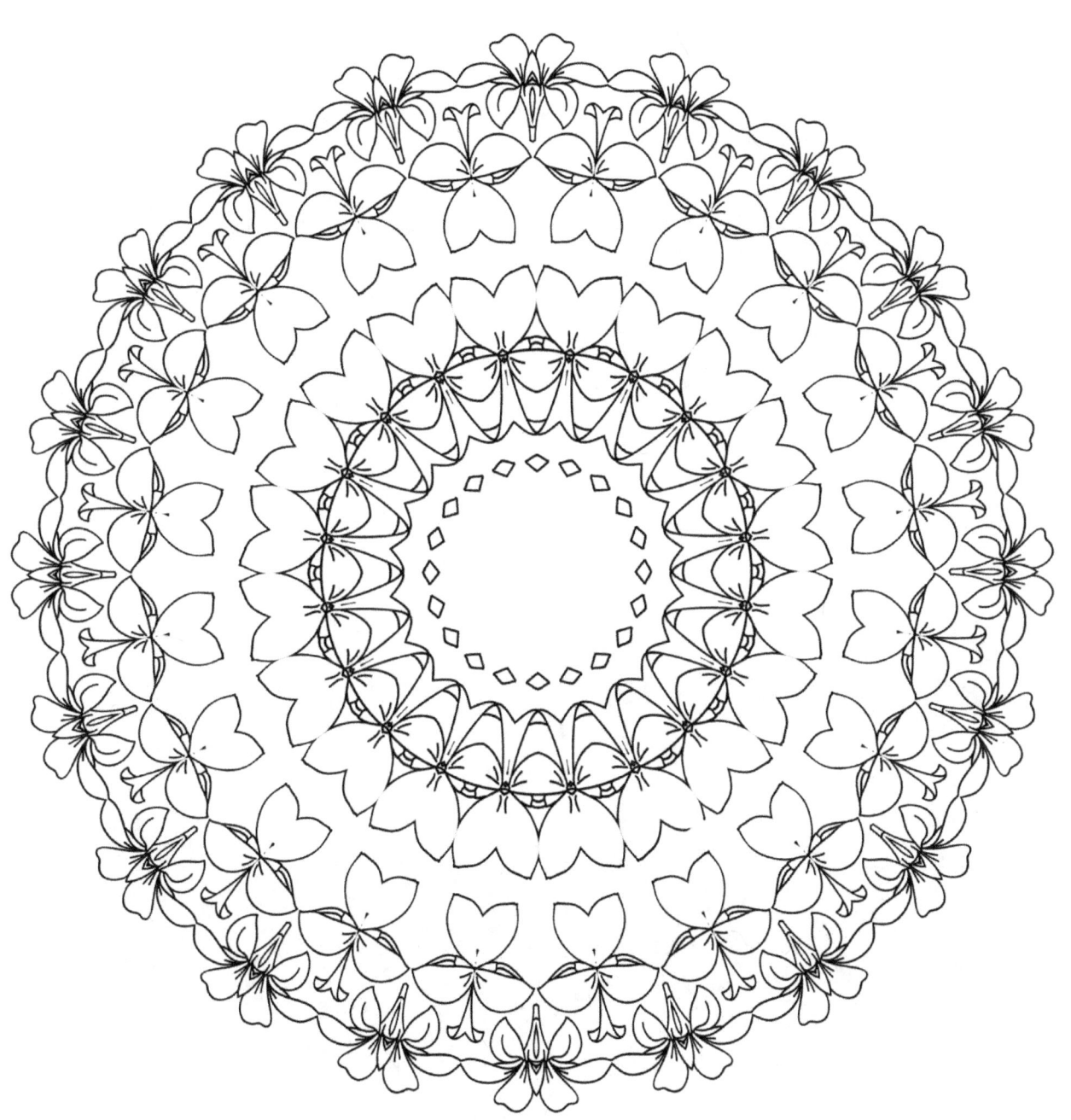

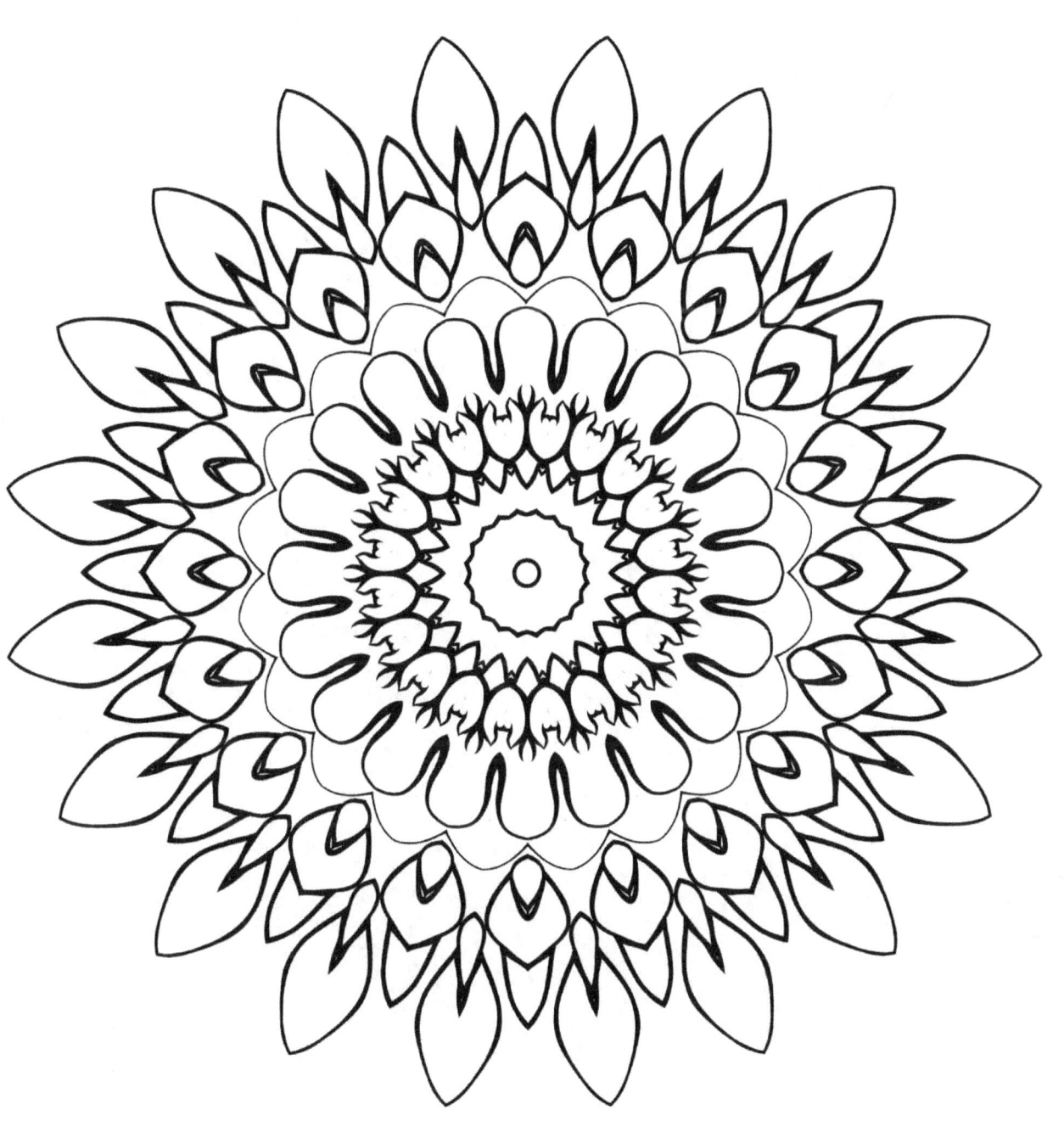

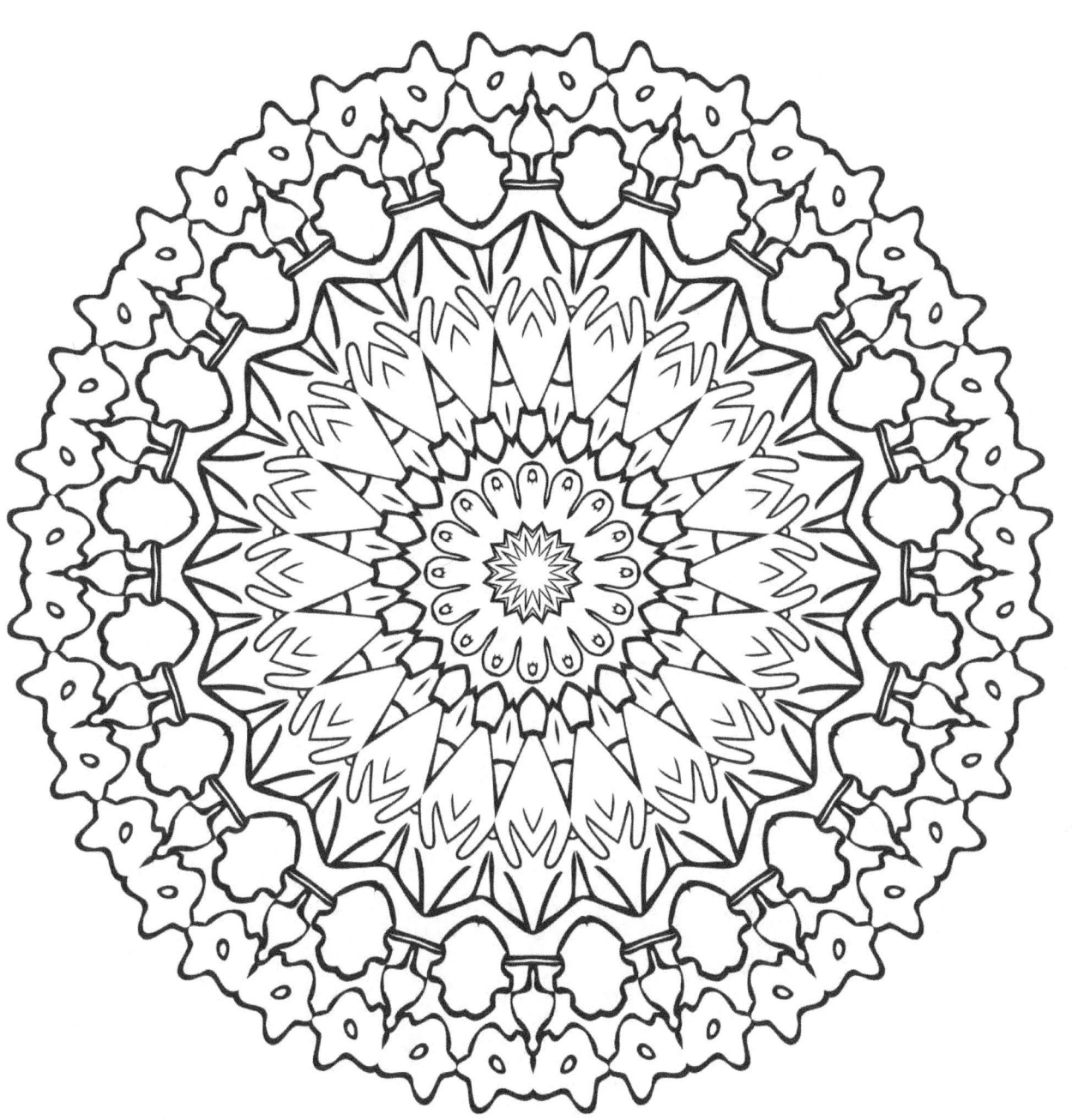

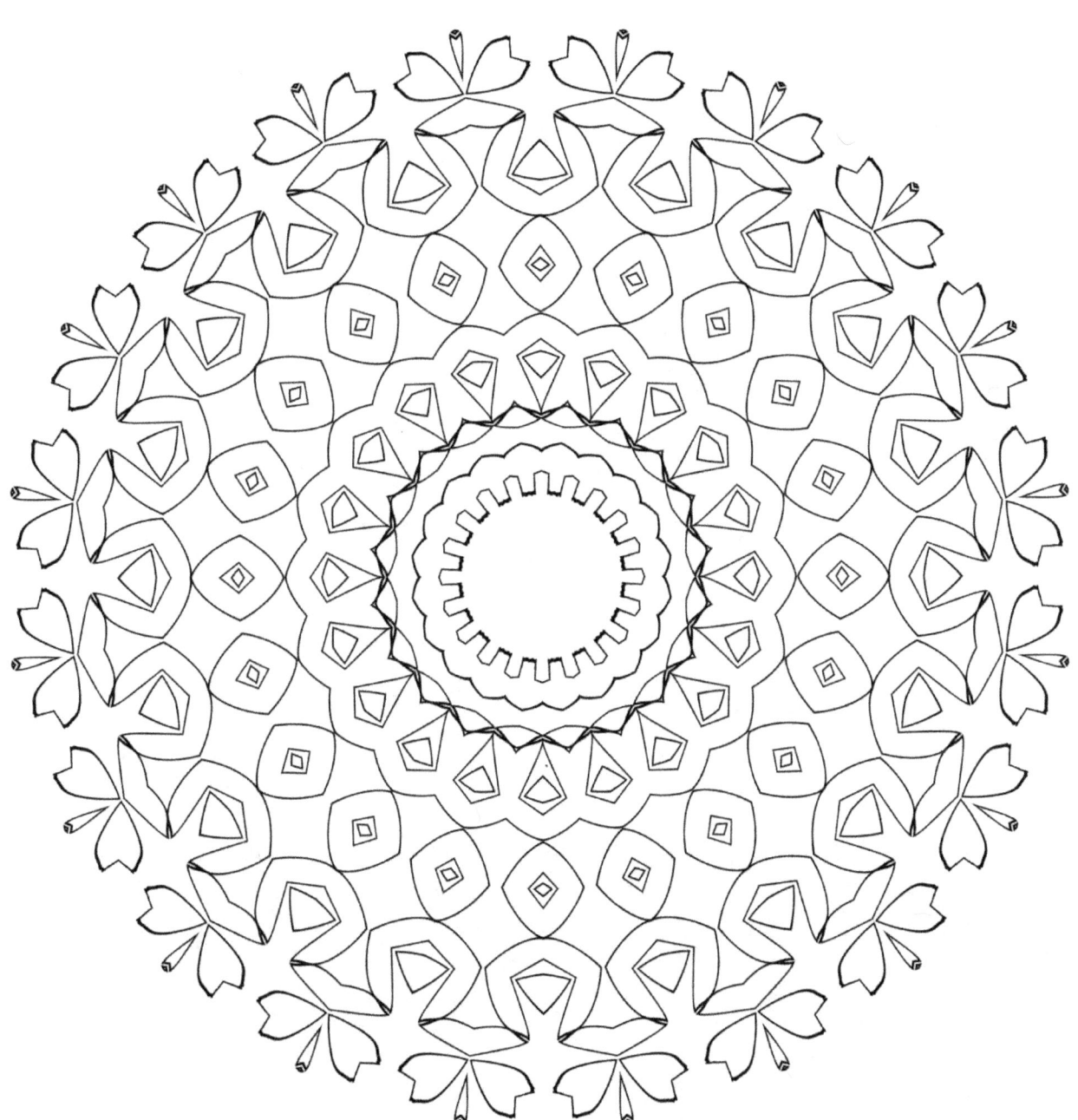

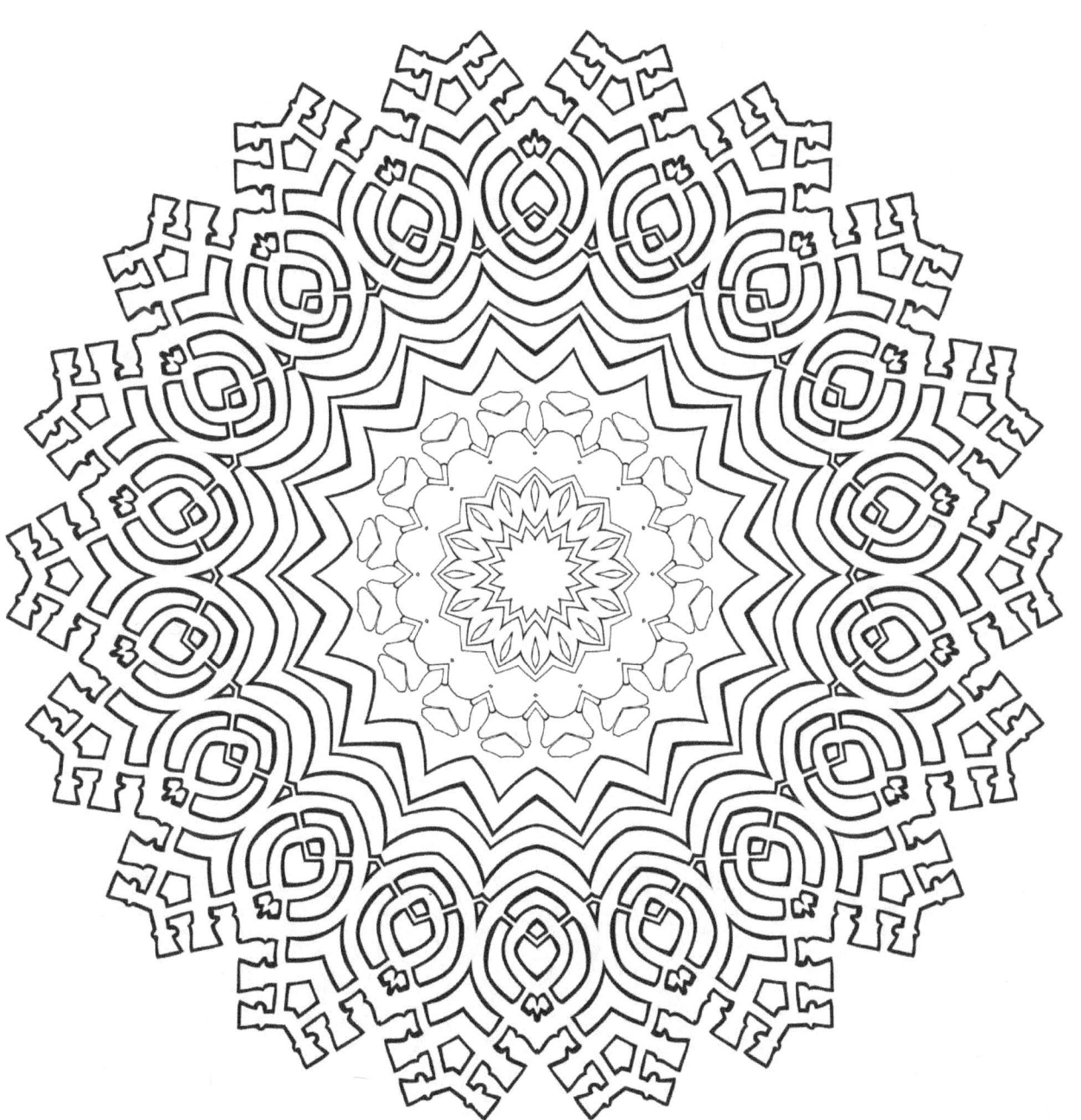

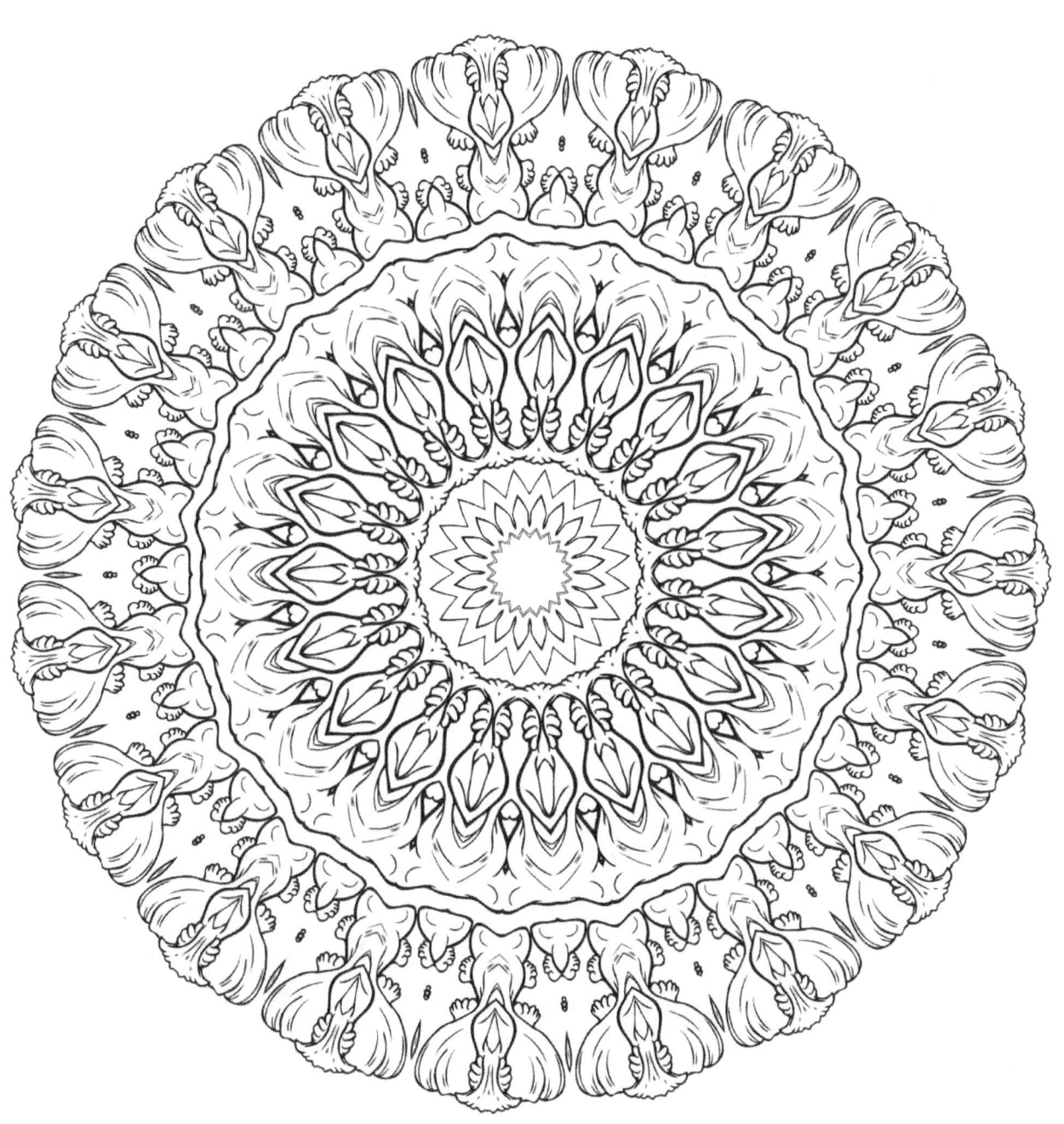

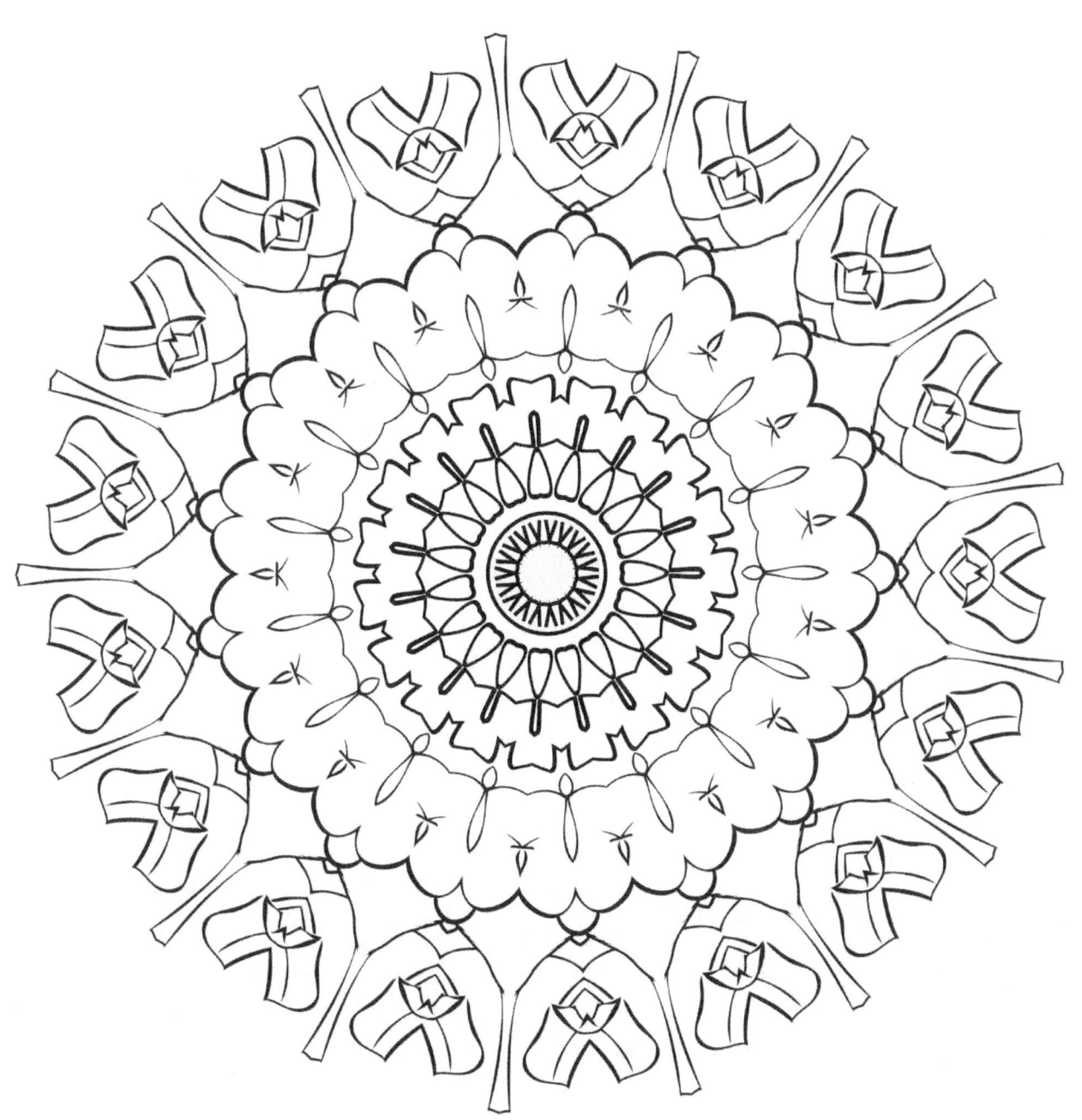

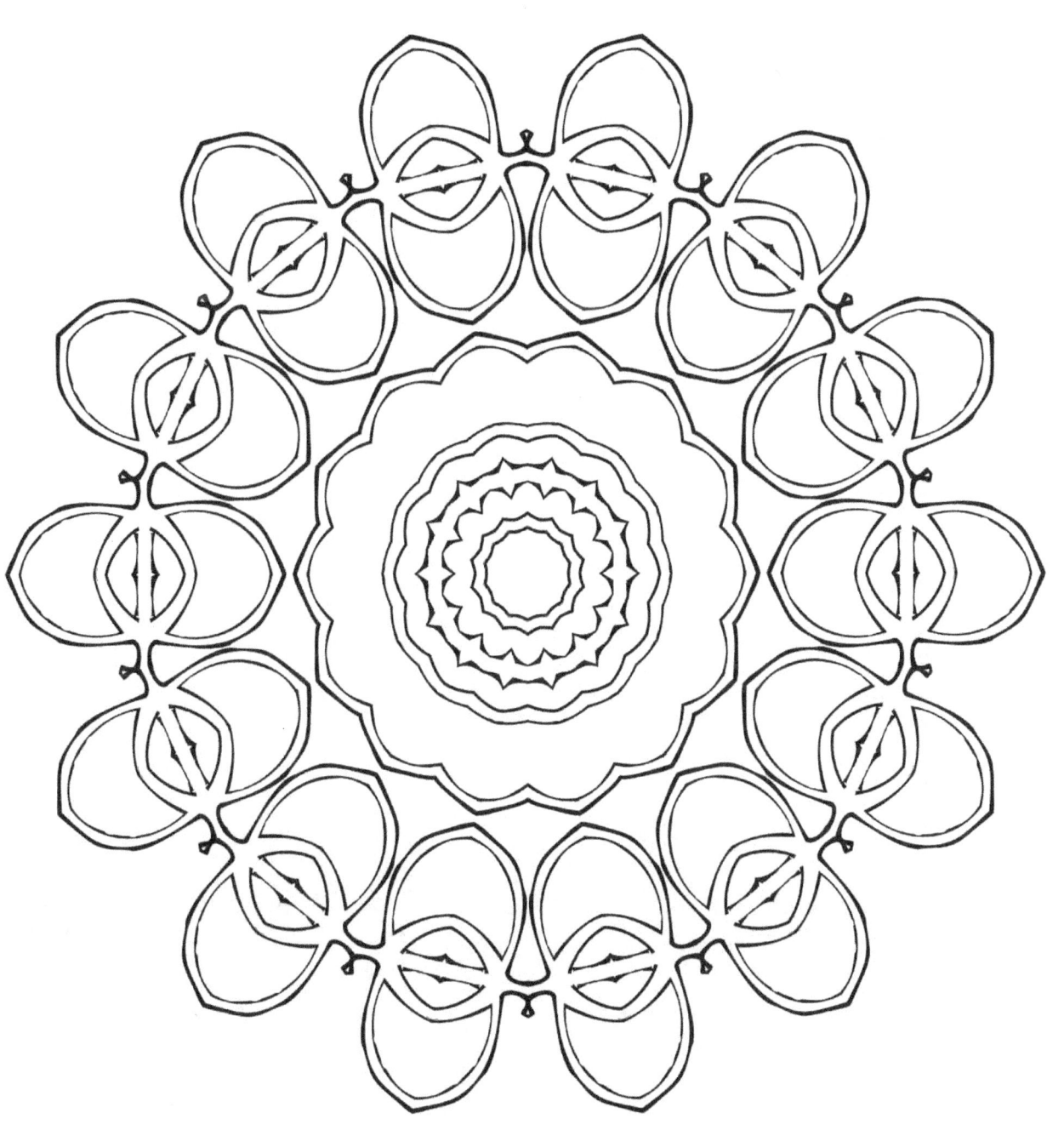

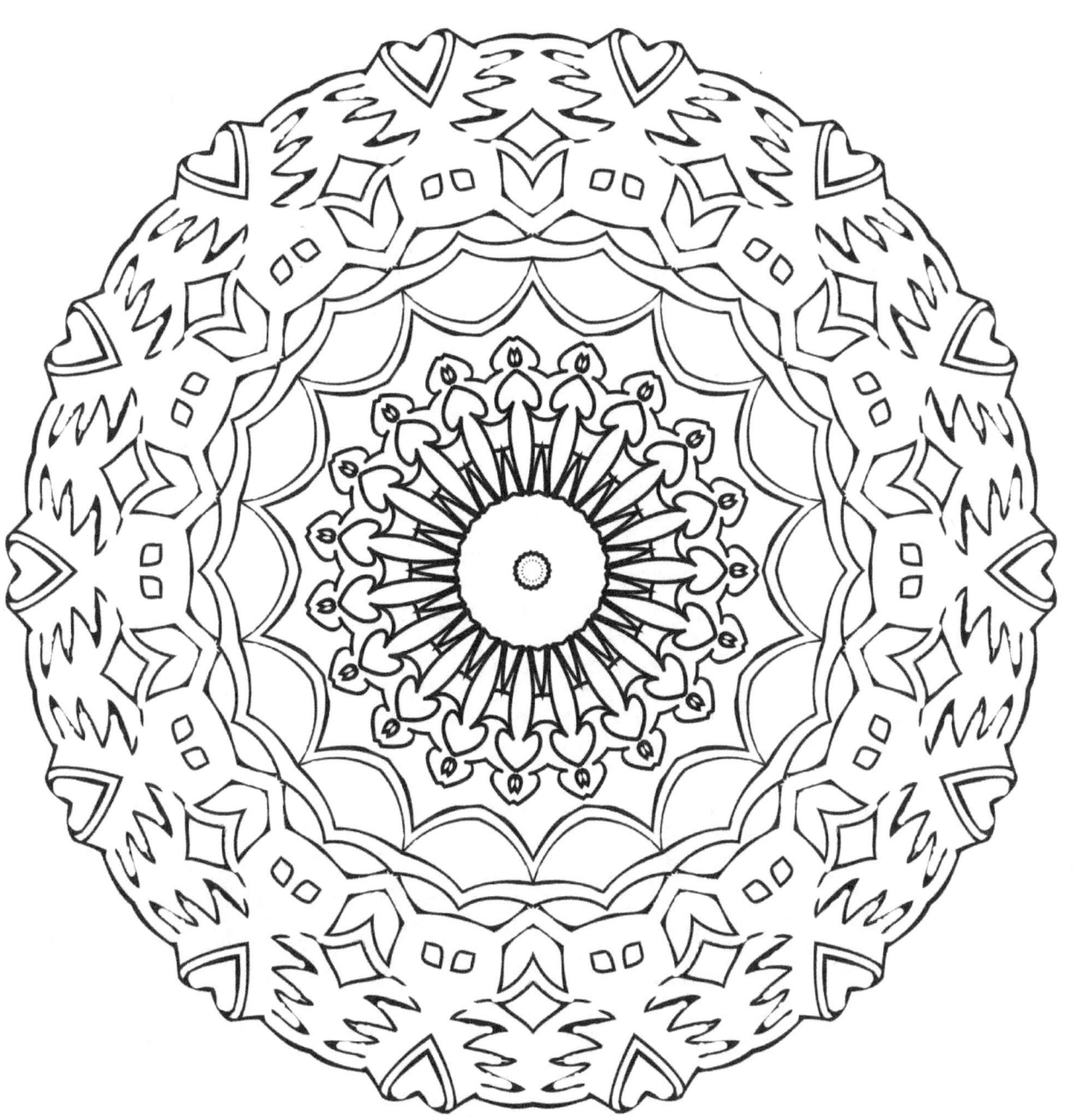

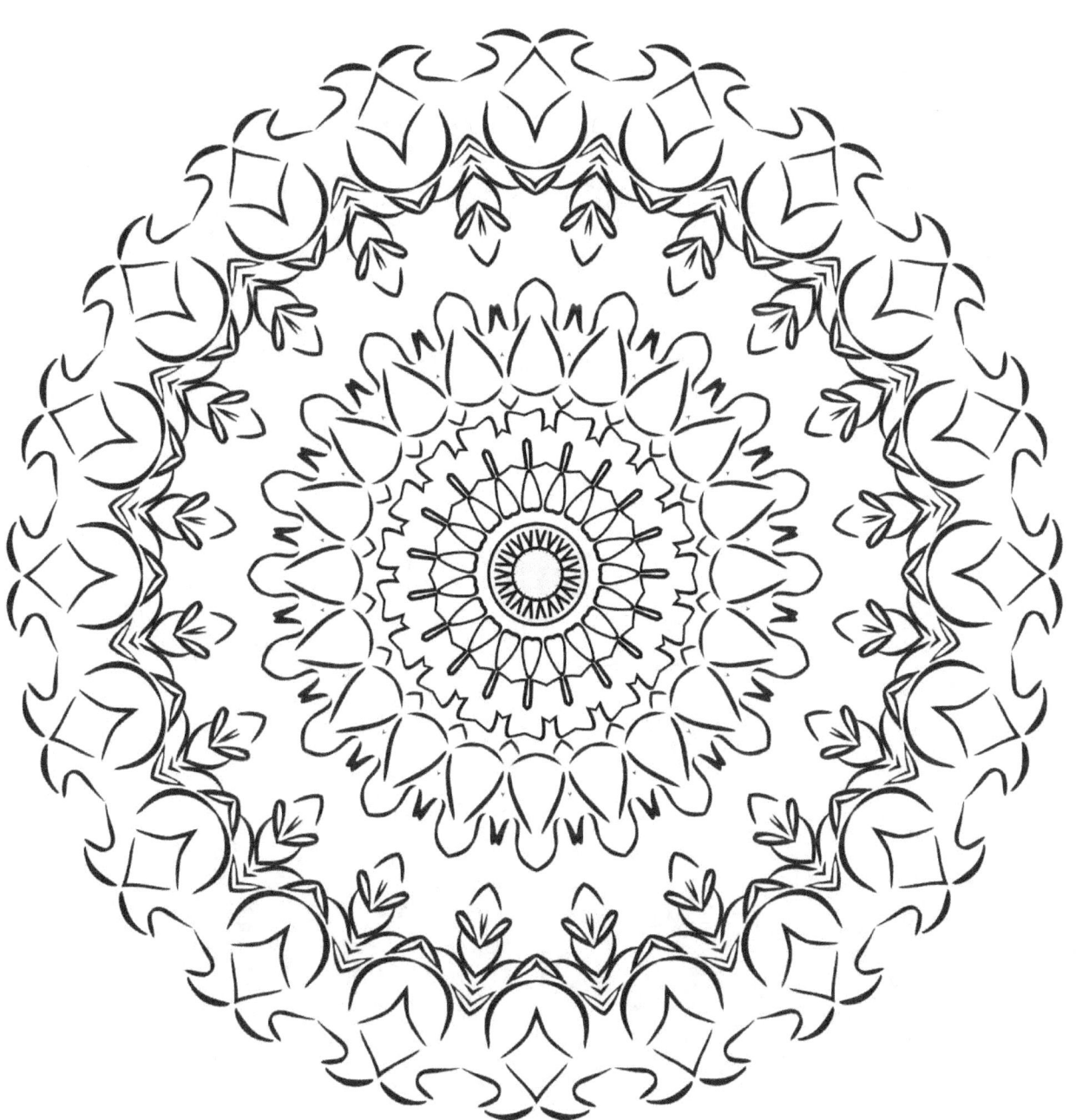

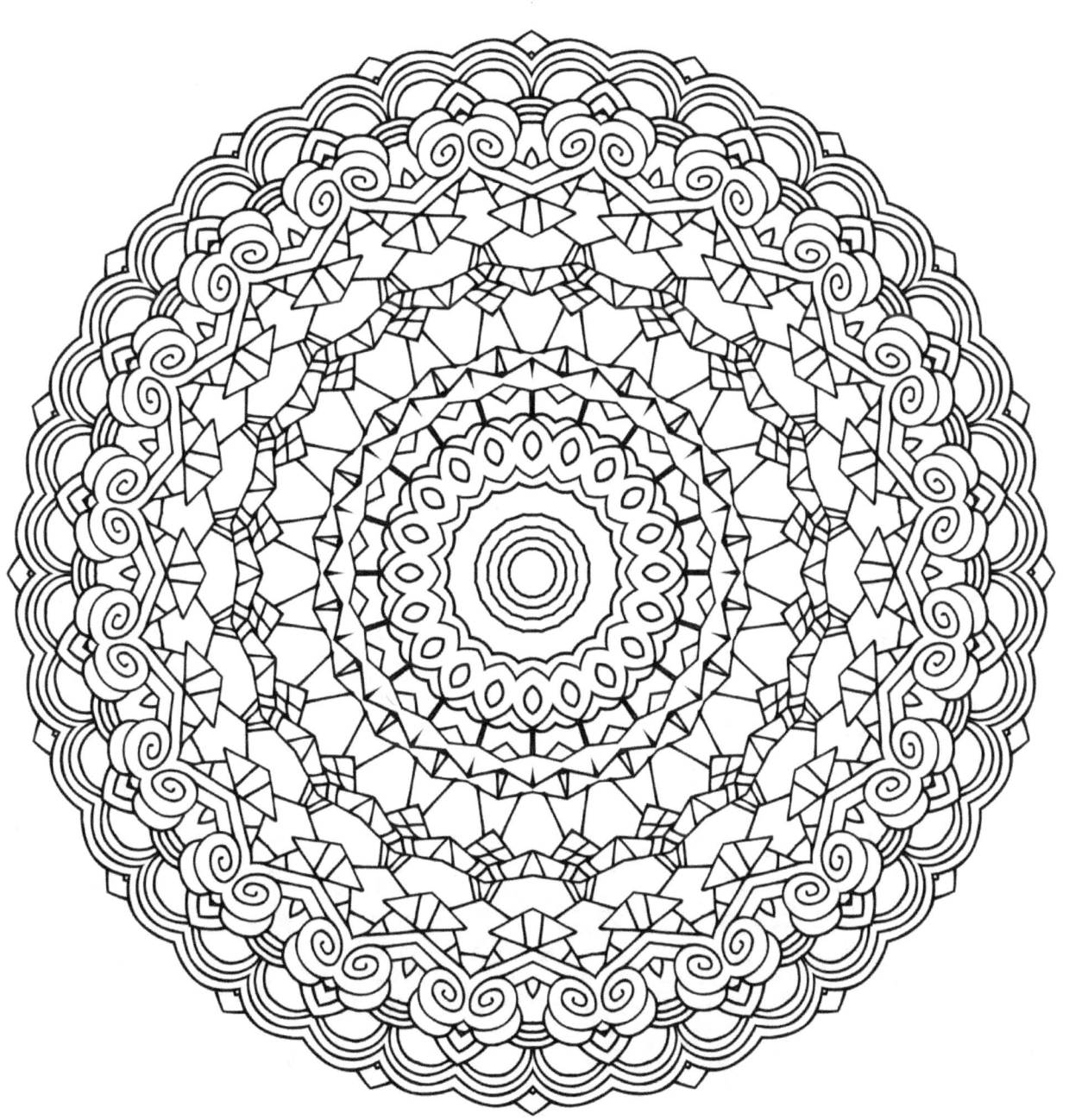

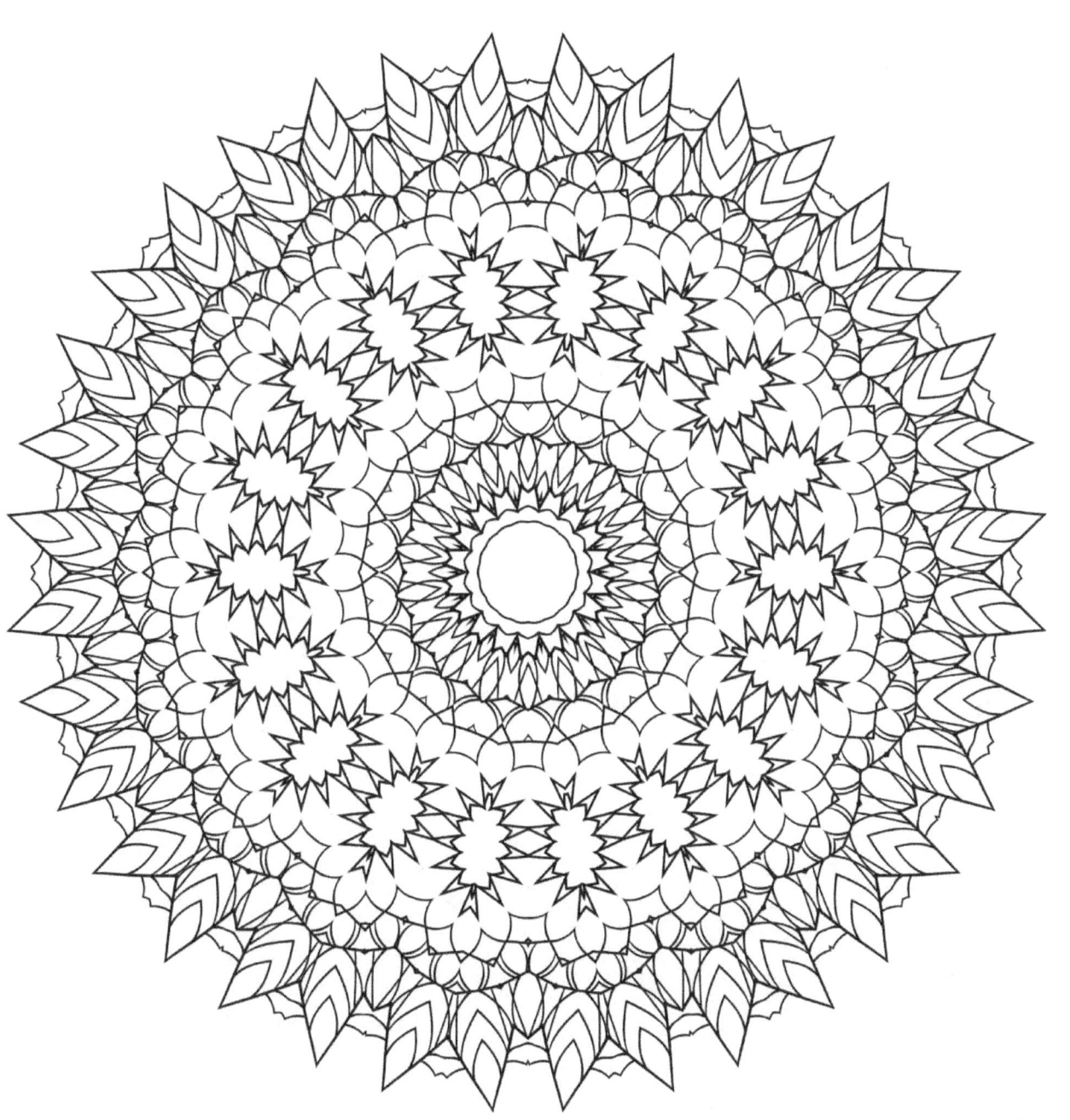

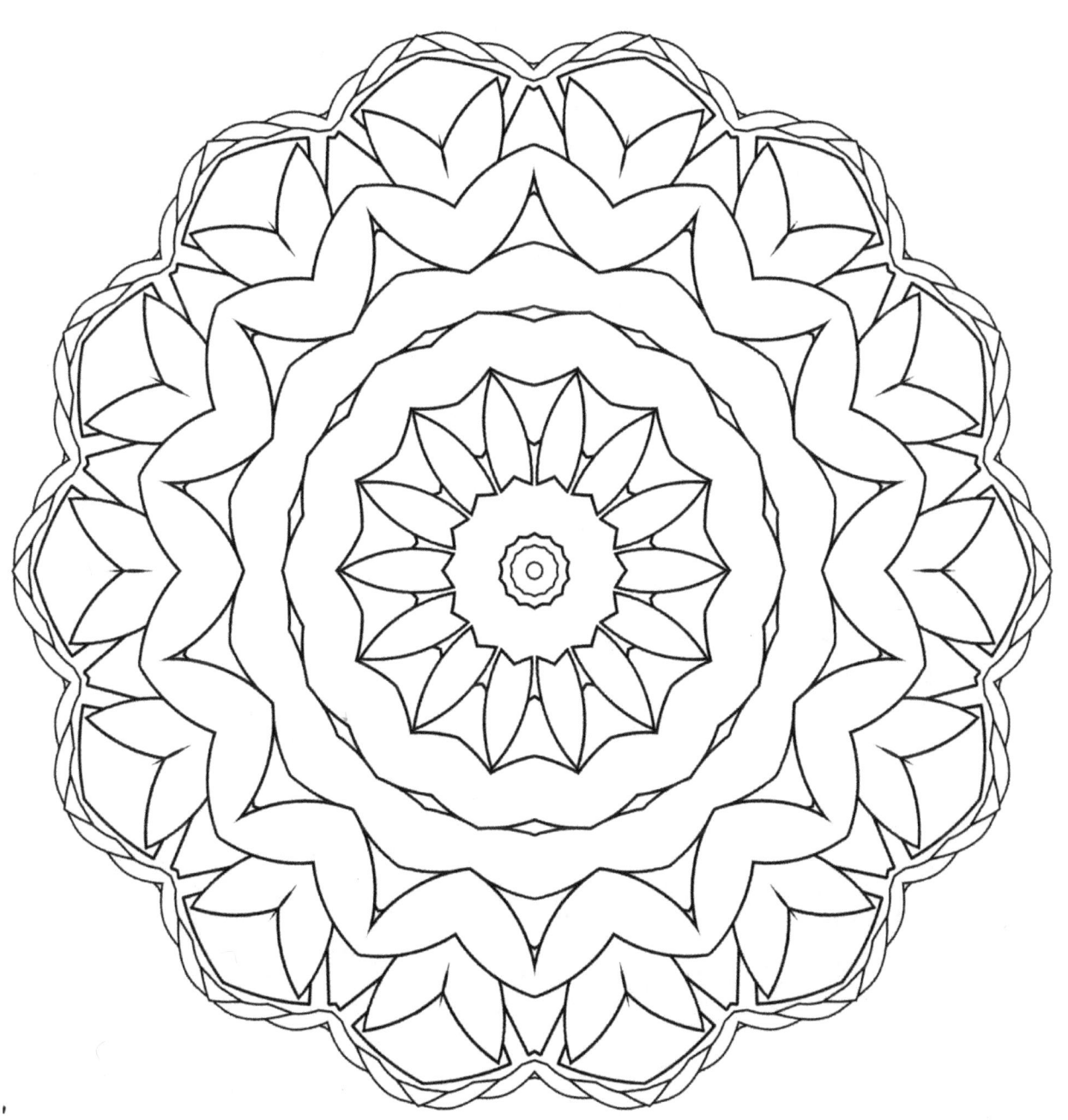

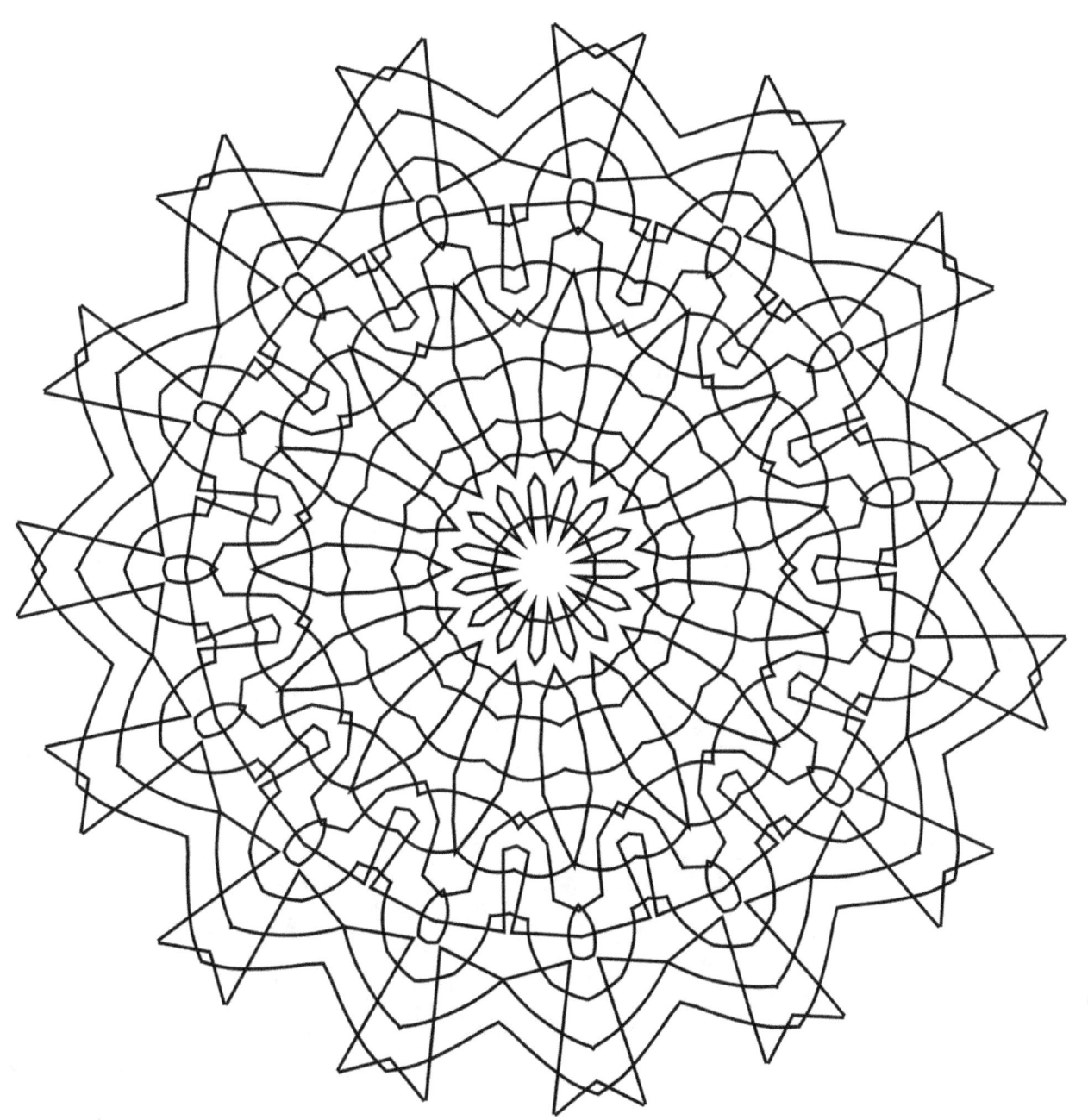